Chemistry 1

*Foundation Skills
for 11-14 year olds*

Bob McDuell BSc

Deputy Headmaster,
Berry Hill High School,
Stoke-on-Trent

Charles Letts & Co Ltd
London, Edinburgh & New York

First published 1986
by Charles Letts & Co Ltd
Diary House, Borough Road, London SE1 1DW

Design: Ben Sands
Illustrations: Beryl Saunders, Brian Stimpson

© Bob McDuell 1986

ISBN 0 85097 650 2

Printed in Great Britain by
Charles Letts (Scotland) Ltd

Acknowledgements

The author and publishers are grateful to the
following for permission to reproduce
photographs and extracts in this book:
Aerofilms Ltd Fig. 15.3 p 56, Fig. 24.2 p 88;
Barnaby's Picture Library Fig. 9.7 p 36; S. Brannan
and Sons Ltd Fig. 4.8 p 21; BOC Ltd Fig. 20.6 p 74,
Fig. 20.7 p 74; British Steel Corporation Fig. A21
p 107; Corning Process Systems Fig. 3.3 p 16, Fig. 3.4
p 16; Crown Copyright Fig. 24.1 (reproduced with
the permission of the Controller of Her Majesty's
Stationery Office); The Distillers Company plc Fig.
11.2 p 43; Philip Harris Ltd Fig. 4.5 p 19, Fig. 16.1
p 60, Fig. 16.2 p 61, Fig. 18.5 p 67; Imperial Chemical
Industries PLC Fig. 15.5 p 59; The Lion Salt
Museum, Cheshire County Council Fig. A24 p109;
The London Transport Museum Fig. 24.7 p 93; The
Metropolitan Police Fig. 12.4 p 48; Oertling
Balances Ltd Fig. 5.1 p 22; The Science Museum
p 13, Fig. 5.2 p 22, p 40, Fig. 23.1 p 84, Fig. 23.3 p 87,
Fig. 23.4 p 87, Fig. 23.5 p 87; The Sunday Times
p 57. Fig. 11.3 p 43 is a Shell photograph.

Preface

Chemistry is an essential part of the curriculum of young people between 11 and 14 years old. It concerns the nature of substances and the changes which they can undergo. In some schools it may be taught as a separate subject. In other schools it may be a component of a Science or Physical Science course. However it is taught, the content and approach are similar and the material is important and relevant. Success in Chemistry at 16+ is a valuable Physical Science qualification and essential for many careers.

Foundation Skills – Chemistry Volumes 1–3 is a series of books designed to introduce young people to Chemistry. Chemistry is a subject which they find fascinating. This fascination explains the large number of Chemistry sets sold as toys each year.

This series of books will provide a unique introduction to the subject. Mastering the contents of these books will go a long way to ensuring success at 16+.

The methods of teaching Chemistry have changed dramatically in the past decade. No longer is it sufficient to learn a large number of facts and to reproduce them on an examination paper. Parents who find it very difficult to understand the work of their children will, I hope, enjoy the new approach.

Emphasis is now given to the acquisition of specific skills and mastering of different concepts. These cannot just be learned but must be developed. The aim of this series is to develop skills and master concepts over a period of three years. The pupil will be introduced to these skills and concepts at the correct level of maturity. It is difficult to monitor the development of individual pupils in a class of 30 and parents can do a great deal at home to ensure that these concepts are mastered and skills are developed.

These books provide, in addition to a clear exposition of basic chemical information, a large number of activities which will help to develop a pupil's basic skills. Some of these activities are practical and can be carried out safely at home using items that are readily available. These activities are shown with an asterisk. Parents or a responsible adult should be involved when practical activities are attempted, especially when substances are heated. Other activities involve the use of practical information in various forms. Some activities are comprehension exercises and others are left deliberately open to stimulate the pupil's imagination.

It has pleased me to know of the successes of a great many students at O level and CSE who have used my book Revise Chemistry. I am sure that success at 16+ can be more certain if the student is prepared for the course.

The project has involved considerable research and discussion. I would like to thank Roy Williams for all his work and advice during the development of the project. I would like to thank Susan and Malcolm Phillips for help with some of the photographs.

I must thank the staff at Charles Letts and Co. Ltd. for their help in the production of this series. Finally I would like to thank my wife, Judy, and my sons, Robin and Timothy, for their great help and patience throughout.

Bob McDuell 1986

4

Contents

Introduction

and guide to using the book

You will find that the Chemistry topics met by a student between the ages of 11 and 14 are covered in the three volumes of Foundation Skills–Chemistry. The approach of every teacher will be different and so the order of topics might be different.

In general terms, Volume 1 is aimed at 11–12 year olds or anyone starting Chemistry.

Volume 2 is aimed at 12–13 year olds.

Volume 3 is aimed at 13–14 year olds.

In Volume 1, the first steps in Chemistry are taken with emphasis given to aspects of safety and chemical 'vocabulary'. This is further developed in Volume 2 but there are the first introductions to some difficult abstract concepts which can cause problems if not mastered at a later stage.

Volume 3 is designed to give a realistic view of Chemistry. The ideas of symbols, formulae, equations and chemical calculations which can cause such problems are introduced. The reasons for studying Chemistry in the upper school to 16+ examination level are also explained. Often 'option choices' are made without sufficient understanding of the relevance of particular subjects.

Much research has been done in recent years into methods of learning and much discussion has been directed at deciding what should constitute a Chemistry course up to 16+. The Assessment of Performance Unit (APU) was set up in 1975 as a branch of the Department of Education and Science (DES). The Unit aims to provide information about the levels of performance pupils achieve in different subjects and how their performance changes over the years.

The terms of reference of the APU are: 'To promote the development of methods of assessing and monitoring the achievement of children at school, and to seek to identify the incidence of under-achievement'.

To this end, in Science, the APU, based at Chelsea College, University of London, and at the University of Leeds, has carried out a large number of tests of pupils aged 11, 13 and 15. The analysis of the results of these tests has enabled the researchers to identify the levels of understanding which we can expect pupils to have at different ages. Foundation Skills–Chemistry, in its three volumes, follows the direction shown by APU.

The Examination Boards have jointly produced 16+ recommended National Criteria for Chemistry which provide guidelines for new examinations in Chemistry at 16+. Foundation Skills–Chemistry takes account of National Criteria in Chemistry.

I am sure parents, teachers and pupils are aware of the importance of supporting work done in school by planned work at home. Present financial restrictions prevent schools buying books for pupils to take home to read. Foundation Skills–Chemistry provides a complete home back-up to work done in school. Success at 16+ very much depends upon firm foundations set at an early stage.

On pages viii–ix there is a skills, concepts and topic analysis table which is a most valuable part of the series. Down the left-hand side of page 8 are listed the various topic units in the book (i.e. contents). Across the top of pages 8 and 9 the various skills and concepts are shown – one column for each. An analysis has been made to show which skills and which concepts are used in each topic unit. The symbol ● means that the particular skill or concept will be needed for that topic unit.

You will notice if you look in all three volumes that the complete range of skills and concepts will not be covered unless the full course is followed. This is because there is a right stage for the introduction of each concept or for the development of a particular skill.

The pupil should work through the topic units in the same order as they are taught in his or her school. Throughout the three volumes the left-hand pages consist of vital information necessary to introduce the different topics. On the facing right-hand pages are the 'Activities' so vital for developing skills and mastering concepts.

Having read through a particular topic unit the pupil should attempt the appropriate 'Activities' section. The 'Activities' are not designed as examination questions. They are intended to practise skills and extend understanding of difficult concepts. They should also be interesting and not too much like homework. When the 'Activities' have been tried the pupil can then compare his or her answers with the answers at the back of the book. Also at the back of each book there is a glossary of chemical terms which the pupil can refer to at any time.

The essential skills identified as important for Chemistry up to 14 and beyond are:

1 Representation by symbols
  A. Reading information from
    I. diagrams
    II. graphs
    III. tables and charts
    IV. classification keys and flow diagrams
    V. chemical formulae and equations
  B. Representing information as
    I. diagrams
    II. graphs
    III. tables and charts
    IV. classification keys and flow diagrams
    V. chemical formulae and equations

2 Using apparatus and measuring intruments
  A. The correct piece or pieces of apparatus for a particular purpose
  B. Accurate measurement

3 Observation
  A. Making accurate observations
  B. Interpreting observations

4 Interpreting and application
  A. Interpreting presented information
  B. Selecting the most suitable statement from a series of statements
  C. Applying a concept to the understanding of new information
  D. Making generalizations from information

5 Designing investigations
  A. Identifying or suggesting statements which can be tested
  B. Planning parts of an investigation
  C. Planning a whole investigation

6 Carrying out investigations. This skill is difficult to practise without laboratory equipment and supervision.

The following concepts are identified as relevant:
  1 Safety
  2 Accuracy and limitations on accuracy
  3 Mixing and dissolving
  4 Separation
  5 Purity
  6 Change
  7 States of matter and their interconversion
  8 Acidity and alkalinity
  9 Elements
  10 Combination
  11 Competition
  12 Oxidation and reduction
  13 Analysis
  14 Particulate nature of matter
  15 Movement of particles
  16 Arrangement of particles (structure)
  17 Atomic structure
  18 The mole, chemical formulae and nomenclature
  19 Economic considerations
  20 Energy

SKILLS

Topic Units	1 REPRESENTATION										2 USING APPARATUS		3 OBSERVATION		4 INTERPRETING and APPLICATION				5 DESIGNING INVESTIGATIONS			6 PRACTICAL
	AI	AII	AIII	AIV	AV	BI	BII	BIII	BIV	BV	A	B	A	B	A	B	C	D	A	B	C	
1 Laboratory safety	●												●	●								
2 The Bunsen burner						●		●			●		●	●	●					●		
3 Chemical apparatus	●		●								●	●					●					
4 Apparatus for measuring	●										●	●	●	●	●		●			●	●	●
5 Weighing	●										●	●	●	●	●							
6 Ice, water and steam	●	●	●				●								●		●	●				
7 Chemical diagrams	●					●					●	●										
8 Mixing											●		●	●			●			●		●
9 Filtration and evaporation	●		●								●				●	●	●					●
10 Distillation											●				●					●	●	●
11 Fractional distillation	●	●									●		●	●	●		●	●	●			
12 Chromatography	●												●	●	●				●	●		
13 Sublimation		●																		●	●	
14 Pure substances		●													●							
15 Where chemicals come from	●	●				●									●	●	●			●		
16 Acids and alkalis		●						●			●	●	●	●	●		●	●				
17 Neutralization													●	●	●		●	●		●	●	●
18 Collecting gases		●				●									●					●	●	
19 Heating common substances								●					●	●	●	●		●	●			
20 Air and its composition		●													●		●					●
21 Processes involving air		●	●				●				●	●	●	●	●		●			●	●	
22 Oxygen						●							●	●	●					●	●	
23 History of discovery of oxygen															●			●				
24 Air pollution		●	●								●		●	●	●		●	●				

Key

1. A. Reading information from
    I diagrams
    II graphs
    III tables and charts
    IV classification keys and flow diagrams
    V chemical formulae and equations

   B. Representing information from
    I diagrams
    II graphs
    III tables and charts
    IV classification keys and flow diagrams
    V chemical formulae and equations

2. Using apparatus and measuring instruments
    A. The correct piece or pieces of apparatus for a purpose
    B. Accurate measurement

3. Observation
    A. Making accurate observations
    B. Interpreting observations

4. Interpreting and application
    A. Interpreting presented information
    B. Selecting the most suitable statement from a series of statements
    C. Applying a concept to the understanding of new information
    D. Making generalizations

5. Designing investigations
    A. Identifying or suggesting statements which can be tested
    B. Planning parts of an investigation
    C. Planning a whole investigation

6. Carrying out investigations

CONCEPTS

1	2	3	4	5	6	7	8	9	10	11	12	13	14	15	16	17	18	19	20		
●																				Laboratory safety	1
●					●														●	The Bunsen burner	2
●	●																	●		Chemical apparatus	3
●	●																	●		Apparatus for measuring	4
	●				●	●														Weighing	5
					●	●													●	Ice, water and steam	6
	●																			Chemical diagrams	7
		●	●	●									●							Mixing	8
		●	●																	Filtration and evaporation	9
●			●	●		●												●		Distillation	10
	●		●	●															●	Fractional distillation	11
	●		●	●								●								Chromatography	12
			●	●		●														Sublimation	13
●			●	●	●	●												●		Pure substances	14
			●	●		●						●						●	●	Where chemicals come from	15
●	●				●		●													Acids and alkalis	16
●							●													Neutralization	17
			●		●	●														Collecting gases	18
	●				●	●			●											Heating common substances	19
	●		●	●																Air and its composition	20
●					●															Processes involving air	21
●					●															Oxygen	22
			●		●															History of discovery of oxygen	23
					●		●											●	●	Air pollution	24

Key

1. Safety
2. Accuracy and limitations on accuracy
3. Mixing and dissolving
4. Separation
5. Purity
6. Change
7. States of matter and their interconversion
8. Acidity and alkalinity
9. Elements
10. Combination
11. Competition
12. Oxidation and reduction
13. Analysis
14. Particulate nature of matter
15. Movement of particles
16. Arrangement of particles (structure)
17. Atomic structure
18. The mole, chemical formulae and nomenclature
19. Economic considerations
20. Energy

Unit 1

Laboratory safety

Most of your Chemistry lessons in school should take place in a laboratory. This is a special room for experiments. It should have supplies of gas, water and electricity. It should also be well ventilated. The word 'laboratory' comes from the Latin word laborare. This word is also the source of the word labour which means to work hard.

A laboratory can be a very dangerous place and it is important to follow the rules which will keep you, and other people, safe. These rules should be displayed on the wall and should include:

▶ Never run around the laboratory.
▶ Keep all exits clear.
▶ Do not leave stools or bags in gangways.
▶ Close drawers and cupboard doors immediately after use.
▶ Never eat or drink in the laboratory.
▶ Ensure fire extinguishers and fire blankets are available and in good working order.

1.1 Protecting yourself

When working in a laboratory you should take care to protect yourself. You should wear an apron or a laboratory coat to protect your clothes. If your hair is long it should be tied back. Eyes, in particular, should be protected by wearing a pair of goggles throughout experiments that may be dangerous.

When using particularly dangerous chemicals you should wear a pair of plastic gloves.

1.2 Safety with chemicals

Many chemicals are no longer used in schools because they are obviously dangerous. In particular, chemicals like benzene which can cause cancer are no longer used. The chemicals we meet in school are not all completely safe. Some are very flammable, i.e. they easily catch alight and burn. Others are poisonous. Copper(II) sulphate, which is widely used in schools, is very poisonous. Fig 1.1 shows labels which you might see on chemical bottles. These labels warn you of possible dangers.

You should always treat chemicals with great care and use them exactly as your teacher tells you. The following rules should be followed:

▶ Never pick chemicals up with your fingers.
▶ Use a clean spatula to remove chemicals from the bottle.
▶ Always put the top back onto the bottle immediately after use.
▶ Clear up any spillage straight away.
▶ Never taste chemicals unless you are told to do so.
▶ Take care when smelling a gas.
▶ Wash your hands thoroughly at the end of the lesson.

1.3 Safety with apparatus

Many accidents that occur with apparatus are very minor. In particular, take care when picking up pieces of apparatus that might be hot. For example, a tripod should be picked up using the bottom of one of the legs.

Never use broken pieces of glassware with jagged edges.

Report all accidents to your teacher.

Fig. 1.1 Warning signs!

Explosive

Toxic

Flammable

Oxidising agent

Corrosive

Harmful or irritant

Activities

Fig. 1.2 What are the likely causes of accidents in this laboratory?

1 Fig. 1.2 shows a scene in a school laboratory. List all the likely causes of accidents in this scene. You might like to redraw the scene with all the dangers removed.

2 In Fig. 1.3, Paula is heating some copper(II) sulphate solution. List the possible dangers in this scene.

3 Safety screens are often used to protect a group of people during a demonstration experiment. Perspex is a clear plastic which is used now instead of toughened glass for making safety screens.

List the advantages and disadvantages of using perspex rather than toughened glass for this purpose.

4 People in different jobs wear protective clothing. For each of the following list the protective clothing that they might use:
Butcher
Building worker
Fireman
Motor cycle despatch rider
Car racing driver

Summary

A laboratory can be safe providing sensible rules are followed. Remember that the biggest source of danger in the laboratory is **you**.

Fig. 1.3 Paula heating a copper (II) sulphate solution. Spot the dangers in this scene.

Unit 2

The Bunsen burner

Heating in the laboratory is usually carried out with a Bunsen burner. This was first invented by Robert Wilhelm Bunsen in 1855. It is a clean way of burning natural gas, coal gas or Calor gas to produce a hot flame (up to 1000°C).

Fig. 2.1 shows the parts of a Bunsen burner. Gas enters the burner through a tube in the base. Air can enter the burner through the air hole but the amount of air entering can be varied by turning the collar. At the top of the chimney the mixture of gas and air burns.

2.1 Steps in lighting a Bunsen burner

(a) Close the air hole.

(b) Turn the gas full on to ensure plenty of gas is entering the burner.

(c) Light the gas at the top of the chimney with a lighted taper.

(d) Adjust the gas tap until the supply of gas is enough for a flame of the required type.

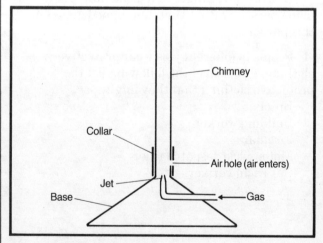

Fig. 2.1 The Bunsen burner

2.2 Types of flame

There are two flames possible with a Bunsen burner. The different flames result from different mixtures of gas and air. The flames are shown in Fig. 2.2 and some of the properties of these flames are shown in Table 2.1.

When a Bunsen burner is alight on a bench, but not in use, it should be pushed well onto the

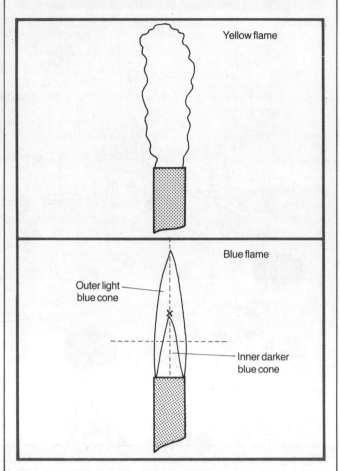

Fig. 2.2 Different flames from a Bunsen burner

bench and left with a yellow flame. It is difficult to see the blue flame, especially in sunlight.

For many purposes a Bunsen burner with the air hole half open produces a very suitable flame.

Yellow (or luminous) flame	Blue (or non-luminous) flame
Obtained when air hole closed	Obtained when air hole open
Irregular shape	Regular cone shape
Cool flame	Hot flame
Quiet flame	Roaring flame
Yellow flame caused by the presence of carbon	Consists of one darker blue cone inside a lighter blue cone
Soot produced by the flame	Inner blue cone made up of air and unburnt gas
	X is the hottest place in the flame

Table 2.1 The two Bunsen burner flames

Activities

Robert Wilhelm Bunsen (1811–1899)

Bunsen was a German scientist born in Gottingen. He studied Chemistry, Physics and Zoology, first in Gottingen and then in Paris, Berlin and Vienna.

He became the Professor of Chemistry in Heidelberg in 1852.

Apart from inventing the Bunsen burner he made many interesting discoveries in Chemistry and Physics.

He carried out research into poisonous arsenic compounds. He found that iron oxide is an antidote to arsenic poisoning.

With G.R. Kirchoff, Bunsen carried out studies of the colours produced when different substances are put into hot flames. These investigations led to the discovery of two new elements, caesium and rubidium, in 1861.

Bunsen invented an ice calorimeter and an efficient carbon-zinc battery. He was the first person to produce magnesium in quantity.

He lost an eye in a laboratory accident.

1 Answer the following questions using the information above about the life of Bunsen.
(a) For how many years did Bunsen live?
(b) How old was Bunsen when he became Professor of Chemistry in Heidelberg?
(c) In which three countries did Bunsen study?
(d) Where do we use carbon-zinc batteries today?
(e) What is the meaning of the word 'antidote'?
(f) What precaution did Bunsen fail to take?

2 Complete each of the following sentences by putting in one of the words in the list.

collar, base, air hole, chimney, jet

(a) The _____ must be heavy to stop the Bunsen burner toppling over.
(b) The amount of air entering the burner is adjusted by turning the _____.
(c) The amount of gas entering the burner depends upon the size of the _____.
(d) The burner is lit at the top of the _____.

3 Fig. 2.3 shows a candle and candle flame. Look carefully at a candle flame and describe each part (labelled **A–D** in the diagram). What can you conclude about each part? You can complete Table 2.2 with your observations and conclusions. What is the fuel for the candle flame?

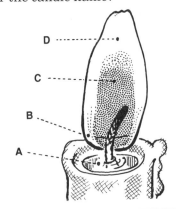

Fig. 2.3 A candle and a candle flame

	Observations (*What you see*)	Conclusions (*What the observations tell you*)
A		
B		
C		
D		

Table 2.2 Candle and candle flame

4 Petrol is a flammable liquid. How could a small amount of petrol in a test tube be heated safely?

5 Kaowool paper is a special white paper which does not burn. When it gets very hot it turns black. What would happen to pieces of this paper if they were held in a Bunsen burner flame along the dotted lines shown in Fig. 2.2?

6 What possible ways of heating apparatus were available in a laboratory before the Bunsen burner was invented?

7 Using an unused match and a pin, how would you show that the inner, darker blue cone is very cool?

Suggest a way of showing that the inner blue cone contains unburnt gas.

Summary

A Bunsen burner with the air hole open produces a hot, blue flame which does not make soot. This is the flame we use most in the laboratory.

Unit 3

Chemical apparatus

The things we use for investigations in the laboratory are called apparatus. In this unit we are looking at some of the common pieces of apparatus that you will meet.

3.1 Apparatus made from glass or clay

Fig. 3.1 shows some of the common pieces of apparatus made from glass or clay. Most of these pieces of apparatus are containers, i.e. they hold chemicals for some purpose.

(i) Test tubes can vary greatly in size. Small test tubes (approx 75 mm long and 10 mm diameter) may be called ignition tubes. Large test tubes (150 mm × 25 mm diameter) may be called boiling tubes.

(ii) A mortar and pestle is used for grinding up large lumps into a fine powder. The bowl is called the mortar and the stick-like grinder is called the pestle.

(iii) A retort is an old-fashioned piece of apparatus.

Fig. 3.1 Apparatus made from glass or clay

3.2 Apparatus made from metal and wood

Fig. 3.2 shows some pieces of apparatus made from metal or wood. Most of these pieces of apparatus are used to hold or support pieces of glass or clay apparatus.

(i) A test tube rack is used to hold test tubes upright when they are not being used.

(ii) Test tube holders are used to hold a test tube during heating in a Bunsen burner flame.

(iii) A tripod is a three-legged metal stand used to support a beaker, flask or evaporating basin during heating. It is used with a gauze or pipeclay triangle.

(iv) Tongs are used to pick up hot objects, e.g. crucibles.

(v) A spatula is a type of spoon used to pick up small amounts of solid chemical.

(vi) A combustion spoon is usually made of iron. It is used to hold small amounts of chemical during burning. These spoons are sometimes called deflagrating spoons. Deflagrating is an old-fashioned word for burning.

(vii) A retort stand, used with a boss and clamp, provides a way of supporting a wide range of apparatus. A wooden stand is used for supporting a burette (Unit 4).

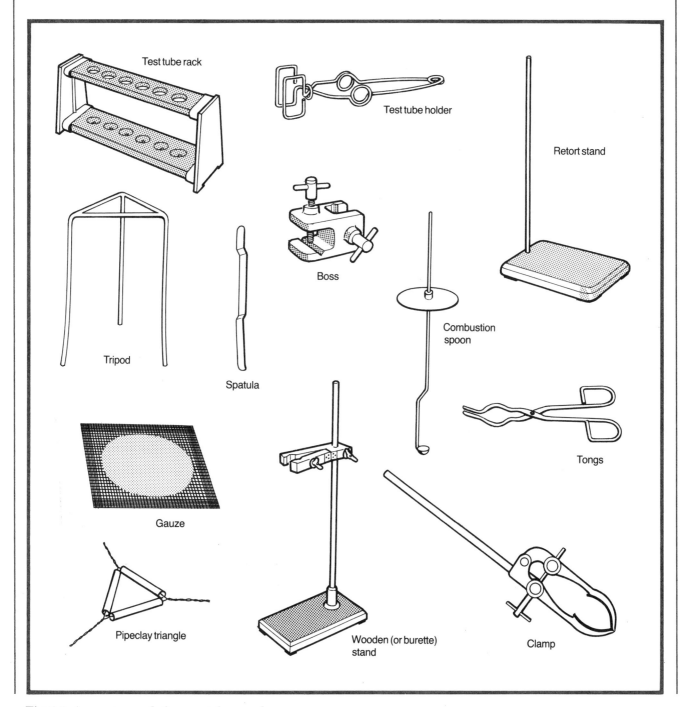

Fig. 3.2 Apparatus made from metal or wood

Activities

1 Which piece or pieces of apparatus in Fig. 3.1 would you use to

 (i) help you to pour some oil into a small hole in a car engine?

(ii) grind some chalk into a fine powder?

(iii) add a few drops of liquid to a test tube?

(iv) heat a small amount of solid?

 (v) hold a few drops of liquid?

2 There are different types of flask. The one illustrated in Fig. 3.1 is called a round-bottomed flask. It is particularly useful when chemicals, especially liquids, have to be heated. Look through the remainder of this book and find other types of flask in use. What are the advantages and disadvantages of these flasks?

3 Beakers can also be made of plastic. What are the advantages and disadvantages of plastic beakers?

4 What are the markings shown in the beaker in Fig. 3.1? How can they be useful in a laboratory?

5 Test tubes vary greatly in price depending upon the type of glass used. Three types of test tube in a Chemistry catalogue were compared. The comparison is shown in Table 3.1.

Type	Size	Type of glass	Price per 100
1	125×16 mm	Soft glass	£3.75
2	125×16 mm	Hard glass	£6.30
3	125×16 mm	Borosilicate glass	£19.77

Table 3.1 Comparing types of test tube

(a) Why is it a fair comparison to take these three test tubes from the lists in the catalogue?

(b) Work out the cost to the nearest penny of a single test tube of each type.

(c) The teacher is planning an investigation in which all the pupils in the class are going to heat three substances in test tubes and observe the changes carefully. At the end of each investigation the test tubes will be so badly damaged that they cannot be re-used. Which type of test tube would you recommend the teacher to use?

(d) Type 3 test tubes are made of glass which is sometimes sold under the trade name of 'Pyrex'. What is the advantage of this type of glass? For what purpose is this type of glass used in the kitchen?

6 Figs. 3.3 and 3.4 show pieces of glass apparatus being made. Explain clearly how the

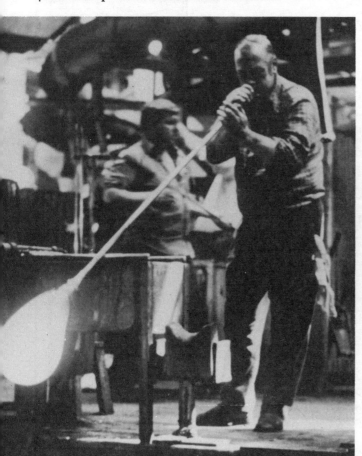

Fig. 3.3 Blowing large containers for sulphuric acid

Fig. 3.4 Making a condenser

following pieces of apparatus can be made:
(a) a flask;
(b) a teat pipette.

7 Many items of apparatus are now made of plastic. For each of the following pieces of apparatus, state whether plastic is a suitable material for making the object. If it is not suitable give a reason, in each case, why it cannot be used.
(a) Retort stand.
(b) Mortar and pestle.
(c) Evaporating basin.
(d) Spatula.
(e) Trough.

8 The following list contains the names of pieces of apparatus with the letters in each name jumbled up. Rearrange the letters to produce the names of six pieces of apparatus.

> **RIBCULEC**
> **RITODP**
> **KERBEA**
> **LAFSK**
> **TASND**
> **TERTRO**

Divide these six pieces of apparatus into two lists:

> **Containers**   **Supporters**
> (hold chemicals)   (support apparatus)

9 Fig. 3.5 gives a 'word search' containing the names of nine pieces of chemical apparatus. In order to find the names you can go horizontally, vertically or diagonally, but always in a straight line.

```
E  N  K  V  E  I  D  H
S  G  S  R  D  P  N  D
S  P  A  T  U  L  A  O
O  E  L  U  R  D  T  P
B  Y  F  R  Z  R  S  I
F  X  O  N  O  E  A  R
E  B  U  T  T  S  E  T
V  O  E  L  T  S  E  P
C  R  U  C  I  B  L  E
```

Fig. 3.5 Word search

10 Unit 3 contains information about pieces of apparatus that are for a wide range of uses in the laboratory. Pieces of apparatus which are used for measuring are included in Units 4 and 5. If you look through the remainder of this book you will find a number of pieces of apparatus not mentioned in Unit 3. List these pieces of apparatus. For each piece of apparatus, write down the material used for making it and briefly the normal use of the apparatus. You will be surprised how many pieces of apparatus we use!

Summary

There is a wide range of apparatus used in Chemistry. It is important to learn as you go along exactly how each piece of apparatus should be used.

Chemical apparatus can be divided into apparatus which holds chemicals and apparatus used to support other pieces of apparatus. We have called these 'containers' and 'supporters'.

Unit 4

Apparatus for measuring

None of the apparatus in Unit 3 is used when taking measurements of any kind. In this unit we are looking at pieces of apparatus used for measuring volume, temperature or time.

4.1 Measuring volume

In Chemistry measurements are based on the metric system.

Remember

1 metre (1 m) = 10 decimetres (10 dm)

= 100 centimetres (100 cm)

= 1000 millimetres (1000 mm)

Fig. 4.1. shows a cube with each side 10 cm or 1 dm long. (The diagram is not drawn full size.)

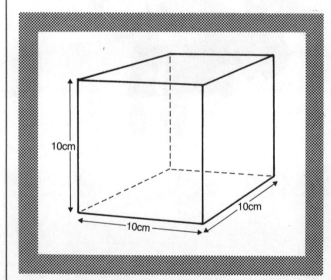

Fig. 4.1 A 10 cm cube

The volume of this cube is

$10 \times 10 \times 10 = 1000$ cubic centimetres

(We multiply the length, breadth and height together. In this case they are all 10 cm.) The abbreviation for cubic centimetres is cm^3.

Alternatively the volume of the cube is 1 dm^3. We obtain this by multiplying 1 dm × 1 dm × 1 dm.

$1 \text{ dm}^3 = 1000 \text{ cm}^3 = 1 \text{ litre}$.

The litre is a unit of measurement used widely in Britain today. Petrol, for example, is bought in litres.

Fig. 4.2 shows pieces of apparatus used for measuring volume.

(i) A measuring cylinder is made of glass or plastic. It can be used to measure out approximate

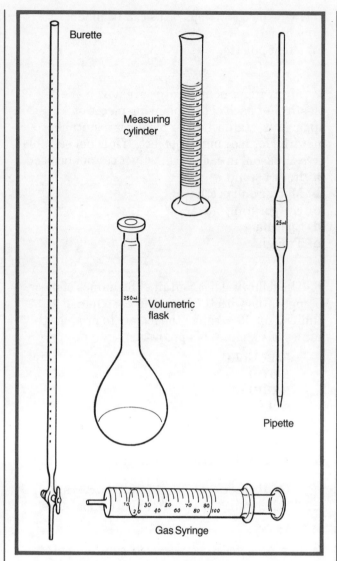

Fig. 4.2 Apparatus for measuring volume

volumes of liquid. It can also be used to collect and measure the volume of a gas (Unit 18).

(ii) A gas syringe is usually made of glass. It can be used for measuring approximate volumes of liquids or gases.

(iii) A burette is used to measure out small volumes of liquid accurately. It is usually supported by a wooden stand.

(iv) A pipette is used to measure out a constant volume of liquid. The same volume can be measured out a number of times. These volumes can be measured out accurately.

All these pieces of apparatus must be very clean. They should be washed out with a little detergent solution and then thoroughly washed out with clean water.

When using these pieces of measuring equipment it is important to have your eye level with the flat surface of the liquid (Fig. 4.3).

4.2 Measuring temperature

Fig. 4.4 shows a thermometer which is used to measure how hot or cold an object is. This is called its temperature.

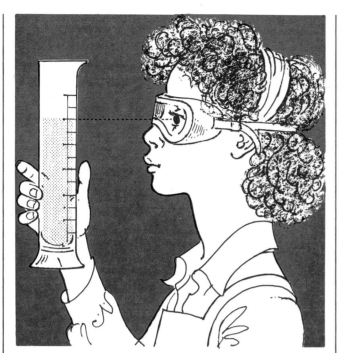

Fig. 4.3 Correct use of a measuring cylinder

Temperature is measured in units of degrees Centigrade (or Celsius) °C.

A thermometer like the one in Fig. 4.4 contains mercury or alcohol. As the temperature rises the liquid expands and moves along the capillary tube.

Should you ever break a mercury thermometer, take care. Mercury vapour is very poisonous.

Many temperatures recorded in °C are negative. For example, on a cold day the temperature may be −5°C. It is possible to record temperatures on the

Kelvin scale and negative temperatures are never obtained. The Kelvin scale is based on the lowest temperature which could ever be obtained. This is called absolute zero and is −273°C. Absolute zero is written as 0 K.

The temperature on the Kelvin scale is obtained by adding 273 to the Centigrade temperature.

  E.g. 25°C = 273 + 25 K = 298 K

It is possible to get thermometers with a dial or digital read-out (see Fig. 4.5).

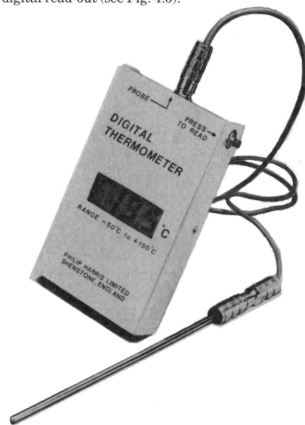

Fig. 4.5 A digital read-out thermometer

4.3 Measuring time

Time is measured in units of hours, minutes and seconds.

  1 hour = 60 minutes
  1 minute = 60 seconds

It is measured using a stopwatch or stopclock. A digital watch will probably be a good instrument for measuring time.

It is now possible to buy an electronic timer similar to those used for accurate timing in swimming or athletics races on television.

4.4 Accuracy

When making measurements of volume, temperature and time it is important that these measurements are as accurate as possible with the equipment being used.

It is important always to give the correct unit with your measurement:

  E.g. 250 cm³, 25°C or 30 s

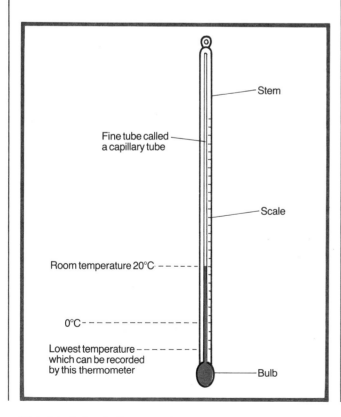

Fig. 4.4 A simple thermometer

Activities

*1 Let us work out the volume of a room in your house. Choose a room which is not too big and fairly rectangular in shape. Use a ruler or tape measure to measure the length, breadth and height of the room in centimetres.

Divide each measurement by 10 to turn your results into decimetres.

Multiply these three measurements together to obtain your volume in units of dm^3. You will probably need a calculator to work this out.

2 Which piece of apparatus in Fig. 4.2 is most suitable for measuring out

(a) $1.3\ cm^3$, $6.2\ cm^3$ and $7.0\ cm^3$ portions of dilute hydrochloric acid accurately?

(b) ten $25.0\ cm^3$ portions of hydrochloric acid?

(c) approximately $40\ cm^3$ of water?

*3 Fresh orange juice is now sold in wax cartons containing 1 litre of orange juice. Measure the length, breadth and height of one of these cartons in centimetres and work out the volume.

Why is your answer probably not exactly 1000 cm^3?

4 You are provided with a measuring cylinder, some water and a pebble. How could you find the accurate volume of the pebble?

Why is it not possible to find the volume of the pebble by measurement?

Why would it not be possible to find the volume of a salt crystal by the same method?

Can you suggest a way of changing this simple experiment in order to find the volume of a salt crystal?

Fig. 4.6 Measuring cylinder and burette

5 All the pieces of apparatus in Fig. 4.2 are only accurate at room temperature.

Why does a liquid give a different volume at 0°C and 100°C?

6 Fig 4.6 shows a measuring cylinder and a burette containing water. Read the volume from each as accurately as you can. You will notice that the water surface is not exactly flat but slightly curved. This is called a meniscus. You should read the lowest point on the meniscus.

7 A class B glass burette with a capacity of 50 cm^3 costs approximately £5. Why is this relatively simple piece of apparatus so expensive?

8 A pipette can be filled by sucking the liquid up with the mouth.

What are the dangers of doing this?
What is the alternative to doing this?

9 You are provided with a long, narrow test tube, some small rubber bands, plasticine, a burette and stand and some water.

How could you make a simple measuring cylinder capable of measuring out 2, 3 and 4 cm^3 volumes of water?

At home, you might be able to make a simple measuring cylinder which will measure out 5, 10, 15, 20 and 25 cm^3 samples of water. Remember that a medicine spoon from the chemist holds exactly 5 cm^3.

10 Measuring cylinders often get broken because they either get knocked over or they roll off the bench and break on hitting the floor. Can you suggest any design points for a glass measuring cylinder which might prevent these breakages?

11 Fig. 4.7 shows parts of two thermometers. Read the temperatures shown on the two

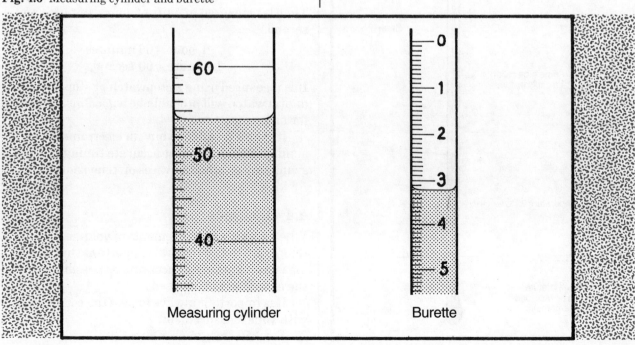

Measuring cylinder   Burette

thermometers. Which thermometer is measuring the temperature of your bath water?

12 Thermometers often roll off the bench and get broken.

(a) What could be done in the design of a thermometer to make this type of breakage less likely?

(b) What can you do during practical work to prevent this kind of breakage?

13 John, without asking the teacher, decides to find the temperature of a hot Bunsen burner

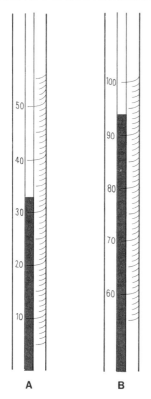

Fig. 4.7 Two thermometers in use

flame. He puts the bulb of a mercury thermometer into the flame and watches the temperature rise. The thermometer bursts and mercury goes over the bench.

(a) Why was this experiment unsuccessful and should never be repeated?

(b) Why was the teacher very anxious to clear up the remains of the broken thermometer quickly?

*14 Using a stopwatch or a watch or clock with a second hand, time various things. For example, how long does it take for the kettle to boil when filled with water and then when it is half filled with water?

Try to estimate a minute without looking at your watch or clock. With practice you can become very good at estimating time.

Summary

There are various pieces of apparatus you will meet for measuring volume, temperature and time.

Items of equipment for measuring volume include:

Accurate – burette, pipette, volumetric flask
Approximate – measuring cylinder, gas syringe

These pieces of equipment must be very clean and must be used carefully to obtain the best results. All liquids, except mercury, have a downward curved surface called a meniscus and it is the bottom of the meniscus which should be read. Readings should always be made with the liquid at room temperature.

The volume is measured in units of cm^3, dm^3 or litres.

$1 \, dm^3 = 1000 \, cm^3 = 1$ litre

Temperature is measured with a thermometer. The bulb of the thermometer must be in the substance, the temperature of which is being measured. The temperature is measured in units of °C or K.

Unit 5

Weighing

In Chemistry we often weigh objects to find their **mass**. The weighing is done on a **balance**. A modern electric balance is shown in Fig. 5.1. Modern balances often have direct read-outs (like a calculator) or a printer which gives you the mass printed on a piece of paper. Some balances can be linked to a computer which will store or display results, perhaps in the form of a graph.

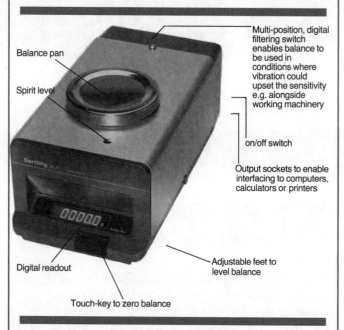

Balance pan

Spirit level

Multi-position, digital filtering switch enables balance to be used in conditions where vibration could upset the sensitivity e.g. alongside working machinery

on/off switch

Output sockets to enable interfacing to computers, calculators or printers

Digital readout

Adjustable feet to level balance

Touch-key to zero balance

Fig. 5.1 A typical modern electric balance

The name 'balance' comes from the old apparatus where a beam was balanced (see Fig. 5.2). Weights were added to the left-hand pan to balance the object on the right-hand pan. This method of weighing required great patience.

5.1 Units

We weigh objects in units of grams (g). A gram is a very small unit. There are approximately 25 g in an ounce.

1000 g = 1 kilogram (kg)

In Chemistry we usually weigh accurately to two decimal places.

The mass changes in experiments are often very small and would not be noticed if the weighing was not accurate.

5.2 Rules to follow when weighing

The following rules will ensure that your weighings are always accurate. Exact details might vary according to the particular model of the balance that you use.

(i) The balance should be plugged into the electric mains and switched on at the plug and at the side of the balance.

(ii) Some balances have a lock to prevent damage if the balance is moved. This should be off.

(iii) The balance should be levelled using the adjusters on the legs of the balance.

(iv) Check that the balance reads exactly zero before anything is placed on the balance pan. You can adjust it to read zero.

(v) Place the object to be weighed on the balance pan. Never put chemicals on the balance pan without using some kind of container. If the outside of a container is wet it should be dried with a cloth. The object being weighed should be cool.

(vi) Do not knock the balance or the bench near the balance during weighing.

(vii) Write the mass down straight away before you have a chance of forgetting it.

Fig. 5.2 Roman bronze balance and ten bronze weights, Pompeii 79 AD

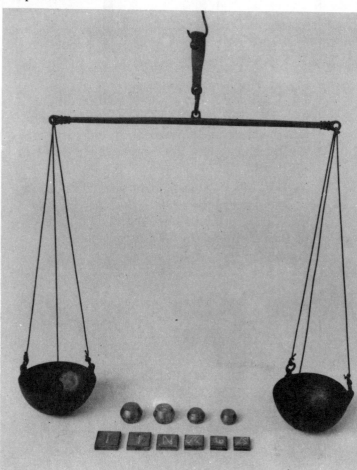

Activities

*1 Estimating is a most important skill. When you estimate you cannot give an exact answer. Estimate the mass of each of the following coins.

> 1p coin
> 2p coin
> 5p coin
> 10p coin
> 50p coin
> £1 coin

Why does a bank cashier weigh bags of coins at the bank?

2 Fig. 5.3 shows Tony doing two weighings. He was told to find the mass of crucible and lid before and after heating with a solid inside. He was trying to find out if there was a change in mass.

Give three reasons why Tony is going to get poor results.

Fig. 5.3 Tony carrying out two weighings

3 Fig. 5.4 shows the read-out on an Oertling TP 31 balance when three objects were weighed. The first mass was 50.65 g. Read the masses of the other two objects.

4 Ether is a liquid which evaporates very quickly. When Lucy tried to weigh some ether in a beaker she found it impossible to get an accurate reading on the balance.

(a) Can you explain why this was impossible?
(b) How would you do this weighing and get an accurate result?

5 Julie weighed a measuring cylinder empty and then she weighed it again containing 40 cm^3 of water. Finally she weighed the measuring cylinder containing 40 cm^3 of a light oil. Unfortunately, although she wrote down the three masses, she got the three masses mixed up. The three masses were:

> 139.75 g   150.47 g   110.53 g

Can you decide which weighing is which?

6 Jane wanted to find the mass of a filter paper but only had a balance which weighed to the nearest gram.

How could she find the accurate mass of a filter paper?
(HINT. A box of filter papers contains 100 filter papers.)

What does she assume when she does this?

Summary

A balance is used to find the mass or weight of a substance. The weighings are made in units of grams (g).

Many experiments in Chemistry require accurate weighings as changes in mass are small.

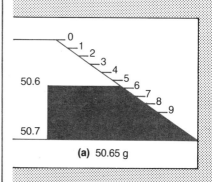

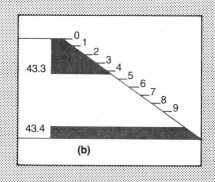

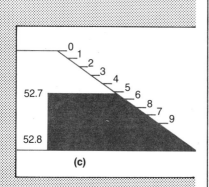

Fig. 5.4 Read-outs on an Oertling TP 31 balance. Object (a) weighed 50.65 g. What did objects (b) and (c) weigh?

Unit 6

Ice, Water and Steam

All substances can exist in three forms or **states** depending upon temperature and pressure. These three states are solid, liquid and gas. Water can exist as a solid (called ice), a liquid (called water) and a gas (called steam).

Figs. 6.1 and 6.2 show water in two states.

In this unit we are going to consider the three states of water.

Fig. 6.1 Ice and water

Fig. 6.2 Water and steam

6.1 Ice

Ice is the solid form of water. It is formed when water is cooled below 0°C. The changing of water into ice (liquid→solid) is called **freezing**. The changing of ice into water (solid→liquid) is called **melting**.

The temperature of 0°C is called either

the freezing point of water
or the melting point of ice.

At 0°C, both ice and water can exist together. A **change of state** is said to occur at 0°C.

If the water is not pure the melting (or freezing) point is lower. Salt is put on the roads in winter to lower the freezing point of water. This makes it less likely for ice to form on the roads. Also, a car radiator is filled with a mixture of water and anti-freeze. The liquid in the radiator does not freeze on a cold day.

When water freezes it expands. This can cause problems if water freezes in a pipe. The expansion may break the pipe.

6.2 Water

Pure water is a liquid between the temperatures of 0°C and 100°C. It is a most remarkable liquid. Life would be impossible without water.

If water is left in an open dish on a window sill the water will slowly disappear. It will take several days. This process is called **evaporation**. It will take place faster in a warm room than in a cold room. During evaporation liquid water is turned into water **vapour**.

When water is heated slowly to about 60°C some bubbles of gas can be seen escaping from the water. This escaping gas is largely air which is dissolved in the water.

At 100°C liquid water turns to steam. This process is called **boiling** and the temperature is called the boiling point. While water is boiling the temperature does not change. Boiling is, in fact, a rapid evaporation which takes place at the boiling point.

The boiling point of pure water does vary slightly from day to day depending upon the atmospheric pressure. If the atmospheric pressure is reduced the boiling point is lower than 100°C.

The boiling point of impure water is slightly higher than the boiling point of pure water.

Fig. 6.3 Where does all this rain come from?

6.3 Steam

Water turns to steam at 100°C and steam is the gas form of water.

When steam is cooled it turns back to water. The steam is said to have **condensed**. This change is called **condensation**. Steam will condense on any cold surface.

6.4 The water cycle

Two thirds of the world's surface are covered by water. This water is constantly evaporating with heat coming from the sun. As the water evaporates it forms clouds of water vapour.

When the amount of water vapour in clouds reaches a certain level and the vapour is cooled condensation takes place. Droplets of rain are formed which fall to earth. If it is particularly cold, the rain might freeze and snow or hail fall.

The rain water eventually returns to the seas by means of streams and rivers. There is, therefore, a constantly repeating cycle. We will never run out of rain!

This cycle is called the **water cycle**. A simple form of the water cycle is shown in Fig. 6.4.

Water is also lost from plants and animals. Most plants lose large amounts of water through their leaves. This water is taken up from the soil through the roots. Some animals lose water to the atmosphere in the air they breathe out and when they sweat.

Fig. 6.4 The water cycle

Activities

1 Liz carried out an investigation with an electric kettle and a thermometer. The kettle had an automatic cut out so that when the water boiled the kettle turned off. She put 1 dm^3 of water into the kettle, put the thermometer into the water and switched on. The temperature was noted every half minute for seven minutes. The results are plotted on the graph in Fig. 6.5 and a graph was drawn.

(a) What was the temperature **(i)** at the start of the experiment and **(ii)** after two minutes?

(b) How long does it take for the water to boil?

Pete repeated the investigation with a similar kettle but without an automatic cut out. The results of his experiment are shown in Table 6.1.

Time (min)	0	½	1	1½	2	4	6
Temperature °C	20	40	60	80	100	100	100

Table 6.1 Pete's results

(c) Plot these results on Fig. 6.5 and complete the graph.

(d) What would the temperature of the water be after three minutes?

(e) Explain why Pete's results are different from Liz's.

*2 When you make a cup of tea it is important to boil the water.

(a) At what temperature should the water be when it is added to the teapot?

(b) Why should the teapot be warmed before the boiling water is added?

(c) Why should the teapot be taken to the kettle and not the kettle to the teapot?

(d) Make a cup of tea for yourself but add the water to the teapot just before the water boils. Are you satisfied with the result?

(e) Mountaineers 7000 m up Mount Everest are unable to make a decent cup of tea using a camping stove. Can you explain why this is so?

(f) Tea and coffee contain a powerful stimulant drug. Can you find out the name of this?

3 It has been suggested by scientists that in the distant future the earth could become much warmer than it is.

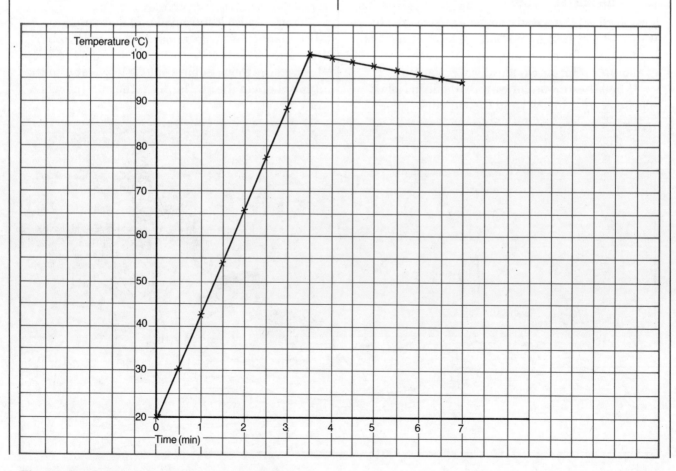

Fig. 6.5 Graph of the boiling of water (Liz's results)

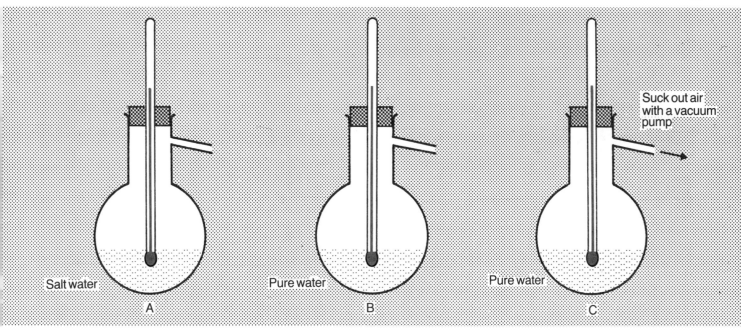

Fig. 6.6 Which of these boils first, and which last?

(a) What would happen to the ice caps around the North and South Poles if this happened?

(b) What would then happen to the amount of water on the surface of the earth?

(c) How would this alter the amount of rainfall on the earth?

4 The three flasks in Fig. 6.6 are heated with identical Bunsen burner flames.
In which flask would the water boil **(i)** first; and **(ii)** last? Explain your answers.

5 Explain each of the following:

(a) A person wearing spectacles finds it difficult to see when he or she enters a hot, steamy kitchen.

(b) Ice forms on the inside of a freezer.

(c) The windows of your bedroom may be steamed up on a cold morning.

(d) Puddles in the road disappear faster on a warm day than on a cold day.

(e) Water from the windscreen washer bottle, when sprayed onto the windscreen on a very cold day, makes it impossible to see out.

(f) Droplets of water may be seen dripping from a car exhaust when a car starts in the morning but not when the engine has been running for some time.

(HINT: When petrol burns water is produced.)

Summary

The three states of matter are:

solid, **liquid** and **gas**

The three forms of water are related as follows:

$$\text{ICE} \underset{\text{freezing}}{\overset{\text{melting}}{\rightleftarrows}} \text{WATER} \underset{\text{condensing}}{\overset{\text{boiling}}{\rightleftarrows}} \text{STEAM}$$

Unit 7

Chemical diagrams

During your Chemistry course you will make a large number of drawings. These chemical drawings are called **diagrams**. It will take some practice before you can draw good diagrams.

Diagrams should be drawn with a pencil and the labelling and labelling lines should be done in ink. Do not make the diagrams too small. Most diagrams look best if they are about 15 cm high. Use a ruler to draw straight lines and compasses or coins to draw circles.

You can buy plastic Chemistry stencils. These can be used to draw the shapes of pieces of apparatus. I do not recommend these to you as they are very restricting. You can only draw the pieces of apparatus certain sizes.

7.1 Section diagrams

In Chemistry we draw section diagrams rather than the three-dimensional diagrams shown in Figs. 3.1, 3.4 and 4.2.

A section diagram is what would be seen if the apparatus was cut in half down the middle. Fig. 7.1 shows section diagrams for a test tube, beaker, flask and funnel.

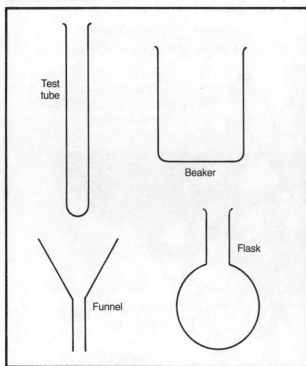

Fig. 7.1 Section diagrams of apparatus

7.2 Drawing supporting apparatus

When drawing diagrams we want to make the important features clear. For this reason we leave out some of the supporting apparatus such as retort stands, bosses and clamps.

Fig. 7.2 shows the way we represent a tripod, gauze and pipeclay triangle in chemical diagrams.

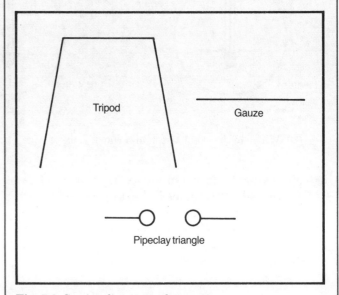

Fig. 7.2 Section diagrams of apparatus

7.3 A Bunsen burner

We do not draw Bunsen burners in all of the diagrams where heat is required. We represent a Bunsen burner with a labelled arrow

HEAT

7.4 A final check

When you have drawn a diagram you should give your diagram a final check before you move on.

(i) Are the different pieces of apparatus drawn to the same scale? You should not draw one piece of apparatus large and another alongside small.

(ii) Are all the pieces of apparatus which stand on the bench drawn at the same level?

(iii) Is the apparatus drawn suitable for the purpose intended? For example, if you are asked to collect a dry gas it should not be collected over water.

(iv) Have you missed out vital corks?

(v) Have you labelled the diagram completely?

Activities

1 Draw section diagrams for the following pieces of apparatus: crucible and lid, watch glass, evaporating basin, mortar and pestle, retort, trough.

2 Fig. 7.3 shows an artist's drawing of a laboratory investigation. Draw a section diagram of the same apparatus.

3 Fig. 7.4 shows a section diagram drawn by Alan of apparatus used to make a gas by heating together a solid and an acid.

(a) Where should the solid be placed in the apparatus?
(b) How should the acid be added?
(c) Where would the gas be collected?
(d) Complete the labelling of the diagram.
(e) Where are the six mistakes in this diagram? Redraw the diagram without the mistakes.
(f) Would this apparatus be suitable for collecting a dry gas?

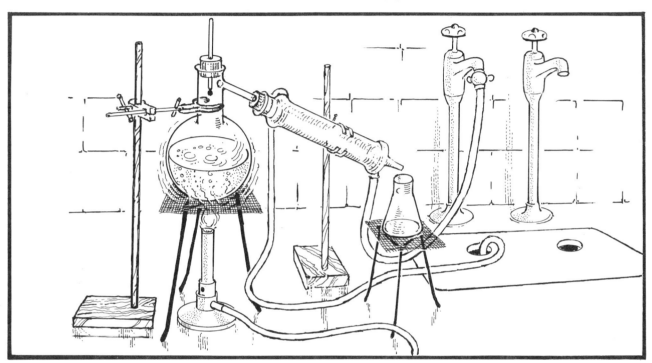

Fig. 7.3 A laboratory experiment

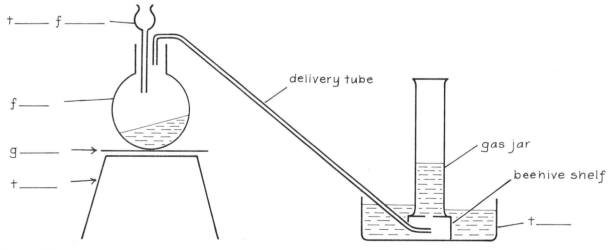

Fig. 7.4 Alan's diagram

Summary

Chemical diagrams are extremely important and can often save many sentences of explanation. They should be clear, well-labelled section diagrams.

Unit 8

Mixing

In this unit we are going to look at ways of mixing substances together. We can call these mixing processes. Also in this unit, and in Units 9–13, we will consider ways of separating mixtures. These are called separating processes. Separation is the reverse of mixing.

8.1 Mixing solids

Solids can only be mixed together well if the solids are finely powdered. When making a mixture of two solids each solid should be ground separately into a fine powder. A mortar and pestle is suitable for this. The two powders can then be mixed on a watch glass using a spatula.

It could be dangerous to grind two solids together with a mortar and pestle.

8.2 Dissolving

When a spoonful of salt is added to water and the mixture is stirred, the salt can be seen to disappear from view. It is not magic, however. The salt is still there and the water tastes salty.

The salt is said to have **dissolved**. The substance which has dissolved (salt in this case) is called the **solute**. The substance in which the solute dissolves is called the **solvent**. The mixture of solute and solvent is called a **solution**.

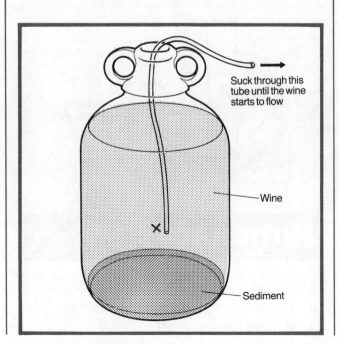

Fig. 8.1 Siphoning off wine

Water is by far the most important solvent. More substances dissolve in water than in any other solvent.

8.3 Decanting

Sometimes a substance does not completely dissolve. The solid which does not dissolve will eventually settle to the bottom and form a **sediment** or **residue**.

During wine-making a sediment forms at the bottom of the jar. Chemicals called 'finings' can be added to speed up the settling out of the sediment.

It is then necessary to remove the clear wine from the jar without disturbing the sediment. This can be done by siphoning off the clear wine (see Fig. 8.1). Once the wine has started to flow it will continue to flow providing the end of the tube marked X is below the level of the wine. Providing the end of the tube X remains above the sediment, the wine can be removed without disturbing the sediment.

For a smaller quantity of solution the same results can be obtained by a process of **decanting**. The sediment is allowed to settle and the solution is carefully poured into another beaker while the sediment remains (Fig. 8.2). If a solution contains some pieces of broken glass at the bottom of a beaker, the solution can be separated by decantation.

This process requires a very steady hand.

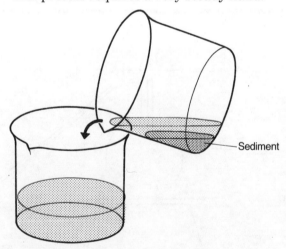

Fig. 8.2 Decanting to remove solution from sediment

8.4 Solvents other than water

Although water is the commonest solvent, there are many other solvents that can be used for dissolving.

(i) Ethanol. This is a useful solvent for dissolving a wide range of plant dyes and inks. It is sometimes sold as methylated spirit. It is useful for removing grass stains or ballpoint pen ink from clothes. It is, however, very **flammable**.

(ii) 1,1,1-trichlorethane. (A very long name! You will meet many similar names in Chemistry.) This is used by dry cleaners for removing dirt from clothes without wetting them.

(iii) Hexane. This is a solvent very similar to petrol and very flammable. It is good at dissolving greasy substances, e.g. candle wax.

8.5 Mixing liquids

Some liquids mix together very well. For example, ethanol and water mix together completely to form a single solution. Liquids which mix together completely to form one solution which is the same throughout are said to be **miscible**.

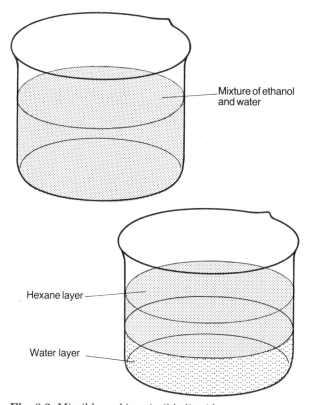

Fig. 8.3 Miscible and immiscible liquids

Hexane and water do not mix, and form two separate layers. The top layer is almost completely hexane while the lower layer is almost completely water. The two liquids are said to be **immiscible**.

The liquid in the lower layer has the greater **density** than the liquid in the upper layer.

It is easy to separate immiscible liquids using a tap funnel (Fig. 8.4).

The mixture of immiscible liquids is placed in the tap funnel. After standing for a while, the tap is opened slightly. The water layer slowly runs out through the tap.

Miscible liquids are much more difficult to separate (Unit 10).

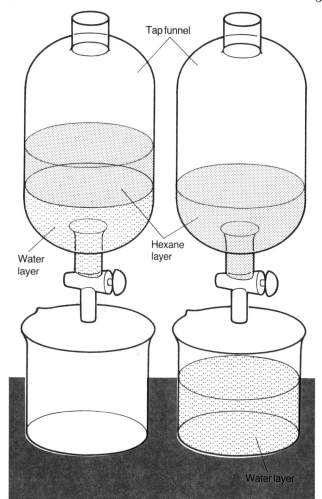

Fig. 8.4 Separating a mixture of hexane and water

8.6 Emulsions

Sometimes two immiscible liquids will not separate out completely into two layers. They may form an **emulsion**. An emulsion is where tiny droplets of one liquid are spread throughout the other liquid. Fig. 8.5 shows what would be seen if an oil-in-water emulsion is viewed through a microscope. Fine droplets of oil are seen spread throughout the watery solution. Chemicals called emulsifying agents present in the solution prevent the droplets coming together and the two liquids separating.

Milk is an emulsion. It looks cloudy and the cloudiness does not disappear on standing. Milk consists of very tiny droplets of fat spread throughout a watery liquid.

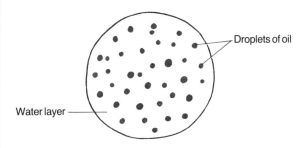

Fig. 8.5 Oil-in-water emulsion

Activities

*1 For this activity you will need similar objects collected into separate piles. For example, you could use a pile of small nails and a pile of small screws. Alternatively, you could use red marbles and blue marbles.

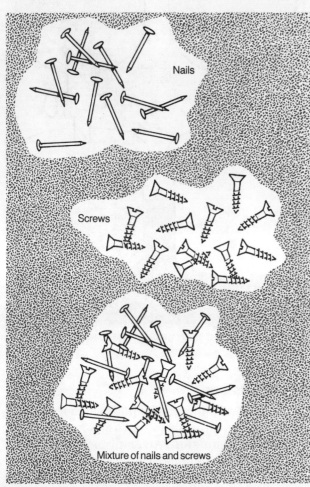

Nails

Screws

Mixture of nails and screws

Fig. 8.6 Separating a mixture is not as easy as making one

Make two separate piles. Then mix the two piles together to form one pile. You have now made a mixture. Separate the mixture back into two separate piles. Is it easier to make the mixture or separate the mixture?

You will find in Chemistry that the formation of a mixture tends to occur easily and is said to be spontaneous. Separating mixtures is more difficult to do.

*2 Completely fill a drinking glass with water and stand it on a working surface. You might notice that the level of the water is slightly above the top of the glass but surface tension stops the water overflowing.

Carefully add salt to the water in the glass and leave the salt to dissolve. Does the water overflow?

Carry on adding salt to the water.

What can you conclude from this simple activity?

(HINT. Imagine that you filled the glass with small glass marbles and added salt. What would happen to the salt?)

*3 Test the following substances in your kitchen to see if they dissolve. Remember you must only add a small amount and stir the water thoroughly.

If a solution is formed it will be transparent and you will be able to see right through it. If you dissolve a coloured substance in water you will produce a coloured solution but it is still transparent.

Substances you can try are: granulated sugar, flour, instant coffee granules, gravy browning, icing sugar, washing soda.

4 You need to dissolve some large crystals in water. Which one of the following would **not** make the crystals dissolve faster?

A. Adding the crystals to water one at a time.
B. Warming the water.
C. Stirring the water and crystals mixture.
D. Crushing the crystals before adding them to water.

5 10 g of salt are added to 100 g of water. The mass of the solution is

A. 90 g?
B. 100 g?
C. 110 g?
D. It is impossible to say?

6 Rock salt is composed of salt and sand mixed together. The rock salt was crushed and added to water.

(a) What apparatus is most suitable for crushing the lumps of rock salt?

(b) The crushed rock salt was added to water and the mixture was stirred.
What happens to the salt and the sand in the water?

7 You are given the task of removing a stain from a shirt. You have a bottle of stain-removing liquid which your mother bought from the supermarket. What precautions should you take when carrying out this task?

*8 Soil consists of a mixture of a wide range of substances. In this activity you can see some of the substances present.

Take a glass jar (e.g. a marmalade jar). Fill the jar with about 3 cm depth of garden soil. Then add water until the jar is about three quarters full. Put the lid back on, turn the jar upside down and shake a few times.

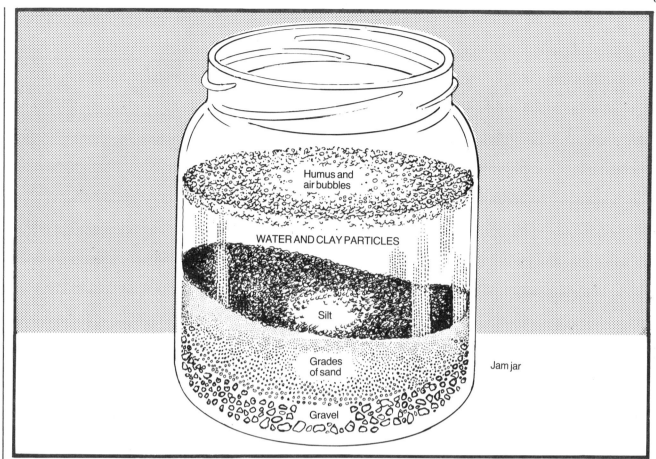

Fig. 8.7 Soil consists of a mixture of substances

Leave the jar to stand with the top uppermost for at least half an hour. At the end of this period compare your jar with Fig. 8.7.

You can repeat this activity with different types of soil.

9 Milk is an oil-in-water emulsion but butter is a water-in-oil emulsion. Explain the difference between these terms.

*10 Look at the ingredients on a bottle of salad cream. Salad cream is an oil-in-water emulsion. A chemical called lecithin acts as the emulsifying agent. This chemical occurs naturally in egg yolk.

*11 Preparing a simple emulsion.
This activity produces a simple oil-in-water emulsion with soap acting as the emulsifying agent.

A few drops of olive oil or cooking oil is added to a jar which is one-quarter full of warm water. Replace the lid and shake the jar thoroughly. You will notice that the mixture goes cloudy. Leave the jar to stand. Repeat the experiment but add a couple of drops of soap solution before shaking. Is there anything different when this is left to stand?

*12 Preparation of a cold cream. This activity requires some co-operation from your parents. Do not use the best saucepan!

The cold cream produced is a simple water-in-oil emulsion.

Weigh about 25 g (or 1 ounce) of beeswax on the kitchen scales. Measure out six tablespoonfuls of liquid paraffin. Add the beeswax and liquid paraffin to a jam jar. Stand the jam jar in a saucepan containing warm water and standing on the ring of the cooker. Stir the mixture with an old spoon until the jar becomes just too hot to hold.

Add two heaped teaspoonfuls of borax to five tablespoonfuls of water in another jam jar. Heat this jam jar until it is also just too hot to hold. Pour the solution of borax in water into the solution of beeswax and liquid paraffin. Stir continuously and continue to stir until the mixture is at room temperature. You should then have produced a simple cold cream.

Summary

Mixing processes occur spontaneously but separation processes occur only with difficulty.

Dissolving is a mixing process. A solute dissolves in a solvent to form a solution. Water is the commonest solvent.

Unit 9

Filtration and evaporation

A *solution is formed when a solute is dissolved completely in water. If sand is shaken with water the sand does not dissolve and a* **suspension** *is formed. The particles of sand remain completely visible. The particles of sand sink to the bottom and form a sediment or residue. The suspension can be separated by decanting (Unit 8). Alternatively, the sand can be removed by filtering or centrifuging.*

9.1 Filtering

Flour in the kitchen may be sieved to remove any lumps. The sieve consists of a fine mesh. The holes in the mesh are small enough to stop lumps passing through. The fine flour grains, however, pass through the holes in the mesh without difficulty.

Filtering or filtration is a very similar process to sieving but with much smaller holes! A filter paper consists of a piece of paper like fine blotting paper. This paper has very small holes through it (about one hundred thousandth of a centimetre diameter). A solution will pass through these tiny holes but large particles such as sand will be trapped on the filter paper.

Fig. 9.3 A centrifuge (the outer metal case on the two tubes containing the mixture has not been shown)

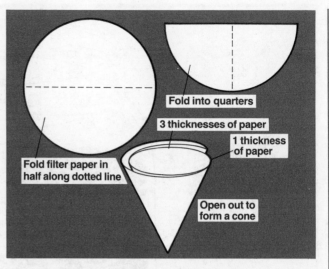

Fig. 9.1 Folding a filter paper

A filter paper is folded into a cone shape (Fig. 9.1) and placed in a funnel to support it. A suspension of sand and water is poured into the funnel (Fig. 9.2). The sand remains on the filter paper and the water passes through and is collected in a beaker. The liquid collected in the beaker is called the **filtrate**.

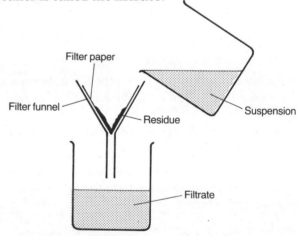

Fig. 9.2 Filtration

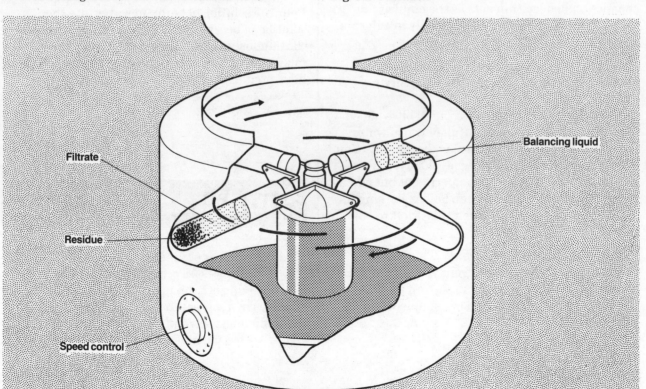

9.2 Centrifuging

Centrifuging is an alternative to filtering, especially if only small amounts of solution are available.

A suspension is placed in a test tube and the test tube is put in one arm of the centrifuge (Fig. 9.3). The opposite arm is balanced with a test tube containing an equal volume of water.

The centrifuge is switched on and the tubes rotate at high speed. Because of this rotation the tubes reach the horizontal position. The particles in the liquid move outwards to the bottom of the tube. The denser solid particles collect at the bottom of the test tube. The clear solution can be removed with a teat pipette.

A centrifuge is used to separate red blood cells from a small sample of blood. On centrifuging, the red blood cells remain at the bottom of the test tube.

9.3 Evaporation

When a salt solution is left standing in a warm room the water evaporates away and salt will remain. This process is very slow.

Evaporation will take place faster if the solution is heated in an evaporating basin so that the water boils away (Fig. 9.4).

It is unwise, as a general rule, to evaporate the solution to dryness as this can lead to the splitting up of the solute.

9.4 Formation of crystals

If a solution is evaporated until only a small volume remains and is then left to cool, **crystals** will form.

Fig. 9.5 shows a crystal of copper(II) sulphate which is formed when a copper(II) sulphate solution is evaporated and left to cool.

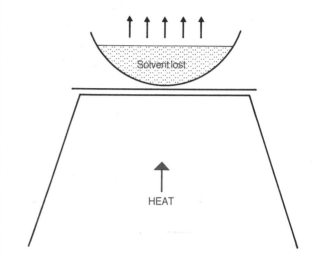

Solvent lost

HEAT

Fig. 9.4 Evaporating a solution

Fig. 9.5 Copper(II) sulphate crystal

Activities

1   Using the information in Units 8 and 9, write an account of the way in which pure salt is obtained from rock salt.

2   The evaporation of a solution was found to be too fast. Using a beaker in addition to the apparatus in Fig. 9.4, draw a section diagram to show how the evaporation can be carried out more slowly.

3   Peter thought his filtering experiment was too slow. He stirred inside the funnel with a glass rod but found the residue was getting into the evaporating basin. Can you explain what his stirring has done?

It is possible to speed up filtration using a Buchner funnel and reducing the pressure in the apparatus with a suction pump. The filtrate is being sucked through the filter paper.

4   Why does a solution in an evaporating basin evaporate faster than a solution in a round-bottom flask?

Fig. 9.6 Filtering under reduced pressure

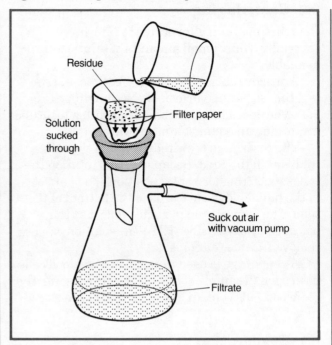

*5   When sugar solutions are evaporated the sugar splits up. We can use this in the making of butterscotch.

Ingredients:
    8 tablespoonfuls (80 cm^3) of water
    450 g of Demerara sugar
    50 g of butter

Fig. 9.7 Settling beds in the Canary Islands showing the large quantities of salt extracted by evaporation of sea water

The water is poured into a saucepan and heated until it boils. The sugar and butter are added and the mixture is stirred until all the sugar has dissolved and the butter has melted.

The solution is brought back to the boil and boiled for two minutes in a covered pan. The lid is removed and the solution is boiled without stirring for a further 12 minutes (or until a little of the mixture, dropped into a cup of cold water, separates into hard, brittle threads). At this stage the mixture is poured into a well-greased baking tin. When it has almost set, mark it into squares with a well-buttered knife. It will then break into pieces when cold.

During the boiling partial splitting up of the sugar occurs. It is difficult to recover sugar from a solution by evaporation.

6 Fig. 9.7 shows the evaporation of salt water to produce salt. The salt water is put into shallow beds and the water is left to evaporate.

(a) Why is this process not economic in Great Britain?

(b) Why is it better to have the salt water in large shallow beds rather than smaller, deeper beds?

7 A mixture of sand and sugar has to be separated. Which is the correct order for carrying out the following steps?
  A. Filtering-evaporating-dissolving
  B. Evaporating-dissolving-filtering
  C. Dissolving-filtering-evaporating
  D. Dissolving-evaporating-filtering
  E. Filtering-dissolving-evaporating

8 Three substances **A**, **B**, and **C** are mixed together. Some of the properties of these substances are summarized in Table 9.1.

Substance	Soluble in water	Soluble in petrol
A	No	Yes
B	No	No
C	Yes	No

Table 9.1 Some properties of three substances. Which could be salt?

(a) Which one of the substances could be salt?

(b) Explain how pure samples of **A**, **B** and **C** could be obtained from this mixture.

*9 Growing crystals.

You should be able to buy potassium aluminium sulphate (sometimes called common alum or potash alum) from a good chemist shop. It is very good for crystal growing.

Dissolve two teaspoonfuls (about 5 g) of alum in five tablespoonfuls (50 cm^3) of hot water in a jam jar. Pour this solution into a shallow dish and leave it to cool and stand for a couple of days. You should be able to find a few well shaped crystals. These crystals are called 'seed' crystals.

Take one of these 'seed' crystals and tie a piece of cotton around the crystal. (This is a difficult thing to do!)

Make another solution of alum in a jam jar. This solution should be at room temperature and as much alum as possible should be dissolved.

Hang the 'seed' crystal in the solution so it is completely covered. Leave the jam jar to stand for some weeks. As the water evaporates the alum crystal should grow.

10 Fig. 9.8 shows a simple crossword. Most of the words you have to find are in Units 8 and 9.

Fig. 9.8 A simple puzzle to solve

Across
  4. Spins test tubes at great speed.
  6. Formed when a solute dissolves in a solvent.
  7. When separating immiscible liquids the liquid with the higher density forms the _____ layer.
  9. A so _____ dissolves in a solvent.
  10. Observe.
  12. It settles to the bottom.

Down
  1. Does not dissolve.
  2. Ethanol and water are _____ liquids.
  3. It helps evaporation of water.
  4. Solids with a regular shape.
  5. Water left in an open dish will _____.
  8. Join metals together.
  11. For example.

Summary

Filtering and centrifuging can be used to separate a residue from a solution.

A solute can be recovered from a solution by evaporation.

Unit 10

Distillation

In Unit 9 we saw that you can get the solute from a solution by evaporation. Salt, for example, can be obtained by heating a salt solution until all the water has gone.

Distillation is a method of obtaining the solvent from a solution, e.g. water from a salt solution.

Distillation is an expensive process because a large amount of heat energy is required to boil the solution. In some parts of the world, where energy is cheap, distillation can be used to produce drinking water from sea water.

10.1 Distillation using simple apparatus

Fig. 10.1 shows simple apparatus being used to get water from a solution of blue ink. The flask is heated until the ink boils. Some small pieces of broken china are put into the flask to make the boiling of the ink steady. The steam that is produced is colourless, not blue.

The steam passes through the delivery tube. As the steam cools down it condenses and turns back to liquid water. When the steam condenses

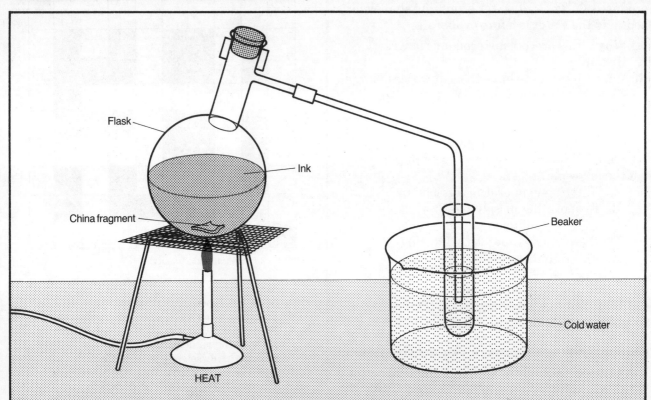

Fig. 10.1 A simple distillation apparatus

considerable heat is given out. The cold water in the beaker aids the condensation.

Even with this cooling water it is not possible to condense all the steam, and clouds of steam will escape into the room.

This method of distillation is not very efficient as it does not condense all the steam.

10.2 An improved apparatus for distillation

Fig. 10.2 shows improved apparatus for getting pure water from some blue ink. The use of a Liebig condenser will ensure that all the steam produced when the ink is boiled is condensed to form water.

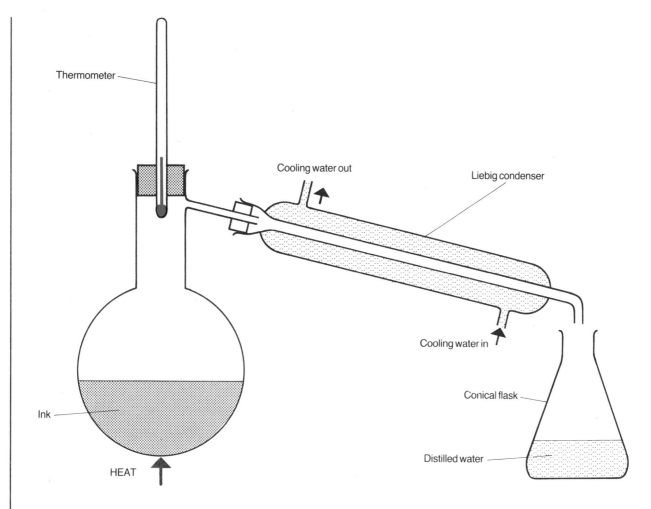

Fig. 10.2 Distillation using a Liebig condenser

The following points should be remembered:

(i) Only steam leaves the flask. The other substances present in the ink remain in the flask.

(ii) The thermometer measures the temperature of the steam. The bulb of the thermometer is alongside the side-arm of the flask and not dipping in the ink. The maximum temperature recorded on the thermometer should be 100°C.

(iii) The Liebig condenser consists of two tubes – one inside the other. Steam passes through the inner tube and cooling water through the outer tube. The cooling water enters at the bottom of the condenser and leaves at the top of the condenser. The condenser must slope downward so that water formed in the condenser runs into the receiver.

(iv) The receiver should be open at the top, i.e. there should not be a cork in the receiver.

The liquid collected in the receiver is called the **distillate**. When water is the solvent the liquid collected is pure water called distilled water.

10.3 Distilled water

Distilled water is very useful for several purposes including:

(i) Steam irons
A steam iron contains a small tank of water. When the button on the top of the iron is pressed water drops onto a heated plate and turns to steam. This steam passes through holes in the base of the iron. The steam helps to remove creases from the clothes being ironed. Distilled water turns to steam without leaving a deposit. With tap water a deposit builds up which will eventually stop the iron working.

(ii) Car batteries
A car battery contains sulphuric acid. In use the water in the acid evaporates. Distilled water is added to restore the original acid level. Tap water contains impurities which rapidly attack the lead plates and stop the battery working.

Many new batteries are being made 'sealed for life'. They reduce water loss and never need 'topping up'.

Activities

1 Fig. 10.1 shows a three-dimensional diagram of simple apparatus for distillation.

(a) Draw a fully labelled section diagram of the apparatus in Fig. 10.1.

(b) Suggest a way of making more of the steam condense without changing the apparatus.

(c) Debra carried out a simple distillation of red ink using this apparatus. The liquid she collected was pale pink. What is the likely explanation for this?

2 You are stranded in the desert miles from an oasis. You only have a spade, a plastic sheet, a few heavy stones and a container – but no water! Suggest a way in which you could keep warm and obtain a small supply of drinkable water. Explain the chemical principles that you use.

*3 You should get some help from an adult before you try this!

You can produce some distilled water in the kitchen using a kettle. Fill the kettle and boil the water. If the kettle has an automatic cut-out you should hold the switch on so that the water continues to boil.

Fill a tall glass with cold water and, gripping the glass at the very top, hold the glass in the steam (Fig. 10.3). Take care that you do not scald yourself.

Cold water

Distilled water

Fig. 10.3 Making a sample of distilled water at home

Droplets of water condense on the glass and drop into the cup. This is distilled water.

4

Baron Justus von Liebig (1803–1873)

Liebig was born in Darmstadt in Germany. He entered university in Bonn to study with Kastner, the most famous chemist of the day. He received the degree of doctor in 1822 and became Professor of Chemistry in 1826.

He was a very hard-working chemist and famous chemists came from all over Europe to study with him.

He did not, as many people believe, invent the Liebig condenser. It was invented by somebody else but it was Liebig's efforts which popularized it.

Liebig carried out many research projects in Organic Chemistry. He isolated several organic chemicals for the first time including trichloromethane (chloroform) and ethanal.

He is also regarded as the founder of Agricultural Chemistry. He showed that certain mineral substances are essential for plant growth. The soil becomes barren unless these substances are added by manure or natural decay.

In 1845 he was made a baron and in 1852 he became Professor of Chemistry at Munich. Much of his work was published in his journal called *Annalen der Chemie* which became one of the major chemical journals.

4 Read the account of the life of Liebig and answer the following questions.

(a) How old was Liebig when he became a professor for the first time?

(b) Name two organic chemicals first isolated by Liebig.

(c) What is the meaning of the word 'isolated' in this passage?

(d) When plants grow they require vital substances for healthy growth.
  (i) How does a plant take in these substances?
  (ii) What happens if these substances are not replaced in the soil?

(e) Why do many chemists in training in Great Britain learn German?

5 Round-bottom flask, Liebig condenser.
  Using the above apparatus, corks, a Bunsen burner and a stand, draw a section diagram of apparatus being used to boil some ink without steam escaping.

8 Fig. 10.5 shows a diagram of a distillation plant in Abu Dhabi which produces nine million litres of pure water a day from sea water.

There are six chambers (labelled A–F). The pressure in each chamber is different, reducing from A to F. The sea water is heated by steam and is then passed through these chambers in turn. Boiling takes place in each chamber and the steam condenses.

(a) Where does the energy come from to produce the steam?

(b) How does the boiling point of water vary in the six chambers?

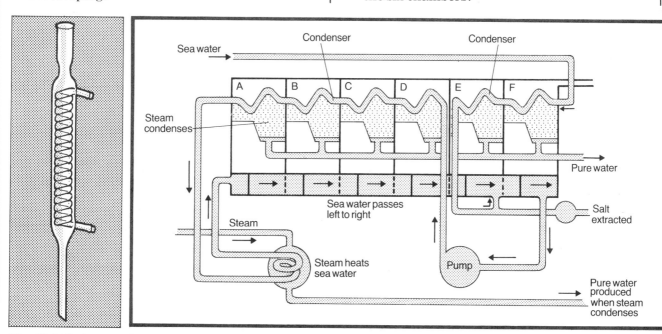

Fig. 10.4 Graham condenser

Fig. 10.5 A distillation plant

6 There are other types of condenser. Fig. 10.4 shows a Graham condenser. Why is this condenser more efficient than a Liebig condenser?

7 Using test tubes, corks, a beaker and glass tubing, draw a diagram of simple apparatus which could be used to distil some water from a solution of copper(II) sulphate in water.

(c) Why does the sea water pass through the condenser before entering the chamber where it is heated with steam?

9 Fig. 10.6 shows a section diagram of a laboratory still. This device enables the laboratory technician to make the distilled water that you use in school. Study the diagram carefully and write a short paragraph explaining how the laboratory still works.

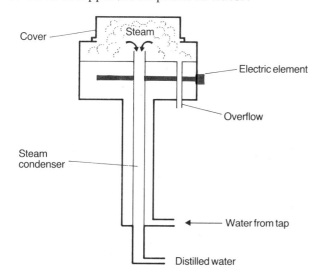

Fig. 10.6 A laboratory still

Summary

Distillation is a method of obtaining a solvent from a solution. The process involves boiling followed by condensation. Efficient distillation requires the use of a condenser. Simple distillation is not suitable for separating a solvent when other volatile substances are present.

Unit 11

Fractional distillation

Distillation is used to separate a solvent from a solid solute. On heating, only the solvent will boil and escape. The solid is said to be **involatile**.

A mixture of two miscible liquids can be separated by fractional distillation, providing the boiling points of the two liquids are not too close together.

11.1 Fractional distillation

A mixture of ethanol (boiling point 78°C) and water (boiling point 100°C) can be separated by fractional distillation.

Fig. 11.1 shows apparatus suitable for fractional distillation in the laboratory.

The mixture to be separated is placed in the flask and small pieces of broken china are put into the flask. The broken china helps to ensure smooth boiling.

The flask is heated slowly with receiver number 1 in place. The ethanol starts to boil first and the vapour passes up the fractional distillation column. Any water which passes up the column condenses and the water drops back into the flask. The temperature on the thermometer remains below 80°C and only ethanol distils over. The liquid collected in the first receiver is called the first **fraction** and consists almost entirely of ethanol.

When the temperature reaches 80°C receiver 2 is put in place and the temperature quickly rises to 95°C. A second fraction is collected.

When the temperature reaches 95°C receiver 3 is put in place and soon a large volume of water distils over as the third fraction.

The results of this experiment are summarized in Table 11.1.

Fraction collected in receiver	Boiling point °C	Volume collected	Ease of burning
1	Below 80	Large volume	Burns readily
2	80–95	Very little	——
3	Above 95	Large volume	Does not burn

Table 11.1 Fractional distillation of ethanol and water

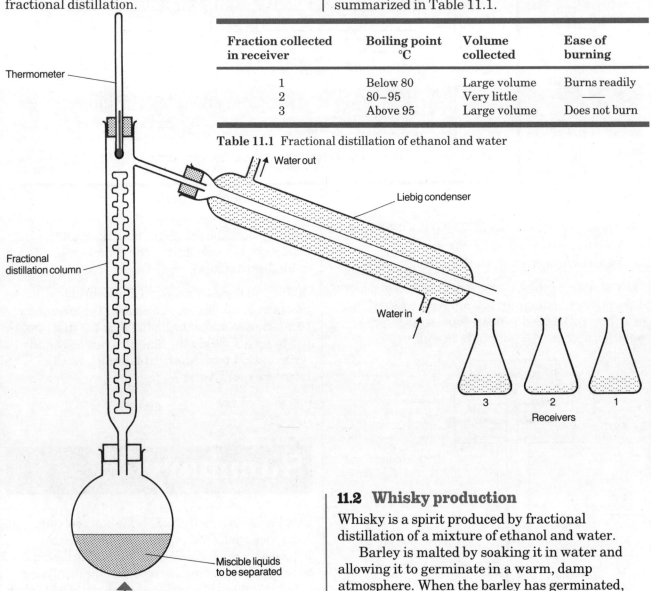

Fig. 11.1 Fractional distillation

11.2 Whisky production

Whisky is a spirit produced by fractional distillation of a mixture of ethanol and water.

Barley is malted by soaking it in water and allowing it to germinate in a warm, damp atmosphere. When the barley has germinated, further growth is stopped by drying the barley in a

Fig. 11.2
Whisky stills

peat-fired oven. The peat smoke gives much flavour to the whisky.

The malt is then ground into a fine powder and the powder is mixed with warm water to produce a sugary solution called 'wort'. The wort is mixed with yeast and **fermentation** takes place. This turns the sugar into ethanol.

The resulting mixture of ethanol and water is then distilled twice in copper fractional distillation vessels called **stills**. The resulting concentrated ethanol solution is stored in oak casks for years in order to mature. During this maturing the whisky absorbs colouring and flavouring from the casks.

Other spirits are made in a similar way but from different starting materials (see Table 11.2).

11.3 Oil refining

Fig. 11.3 shows an oil refinery. In an oil refinery crude oil is split up into different fractions. Crude

Spirit	Source
Whisky	Barley, rye or maize
Rum	Molasses (syrup from sugar cane refining)
Brandy	Grapes
Gin	Grain flavoured with juniper berries
Slivovitz	Plums

Table 11.2 Other spirits

oil is a complicated mixture of a large number of miscible liquids with different boiling points. The fractions produced are not pure substances but each fraction contains substances with similar boiling points. The different fractions can be sold for different purposes.

This process is described in more detail in *Foundation Skills–Chemistry* Volume 3.

Fig. 11.3 Oil refinery

Activities

1 Using the apparatus in Fig. 11.4 plus corks, glass tubing and a Bunsen burner, draw a section diagram of apparatus which could be used to separate two liquids with boiling points of 60°C and 110°C.

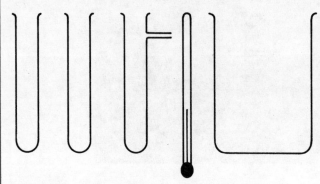

Fig. 11.4 Apparatus for separating two liquids of boiling point 60°C and 110°C respectively

2 Fig. 11.5 shows a graph obtained during an investigation into the separation of a mixture of three miscible liquids by fractional distillation. Every minute the temperature shown on the thermometer was recorded. This is a graph of temperature on the thermometer (on the vertical or **y** axis) and time (on the horizontal or **x** axis).

Study the graph carefully and answer the following questions:

(a) What is room temperature?

(b) After how many minutes does the first liquid start to boil off? What is the boiling point of this liquid?

(c) After how many minutes does the second liquid start to boil off? What is the boiling point of this liquid?

(d) After how many minutes does the third liquid start to boil off? What is the boiling point of this liquid? What is this liquid?

(e) What is the temperature on the thermometer after seven minutes?

(f) Why does the thermometer still show 20°C after two minutes?

There are four points labelled on the graph (**A, B, C** and **D**).

(g) At which point (**A, B, C** or **D**) is
   (i) the temperature greatest?
   (ii) the temperature constant?
   (iii) the rate of temperature change fastest?

3 The strength of alcoholic drinks is often measured in terms of 'degrees proof'. Can you find the origin of the 'proof' system used in Great Britain?

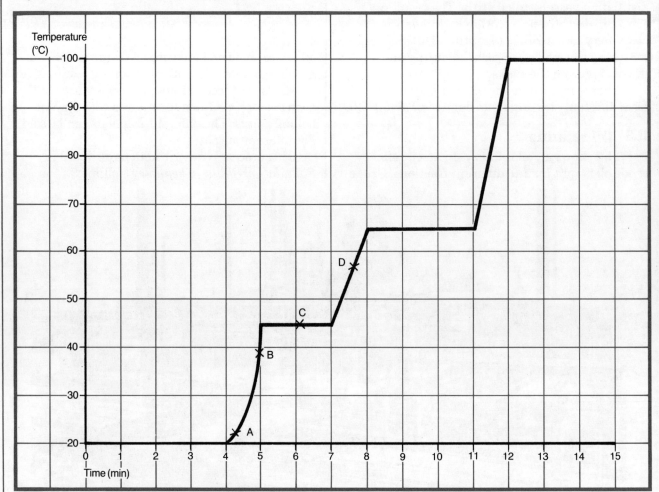

Fig. 11.5 Separation of three liquids by fractional distillation

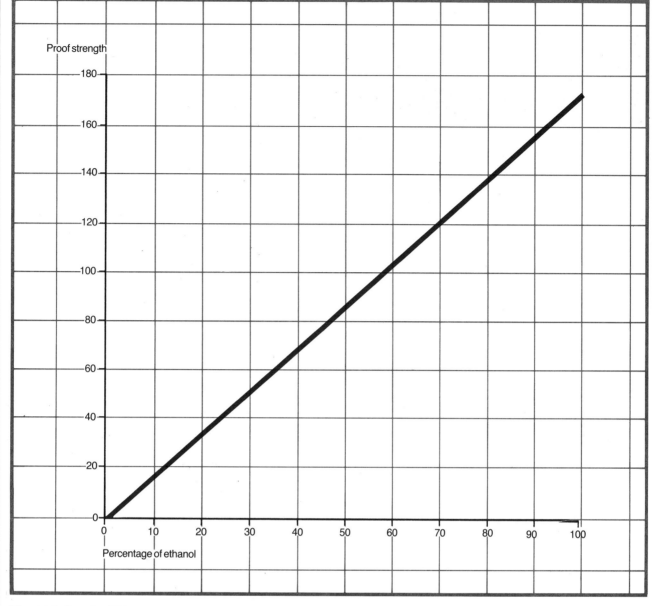

Fig. 11.6 Graph of UK proof strength v. percentage of ethanol

Fig. 11.6 shows a graph of the proof strength (on the vertical axis) v. the percentage of ethanol (on the horizontal axis).

(a) A bottle of whisky is said to be 70° proof. What is the percentage of ethanol in the whisky?

(b) A bottle of wine contains 10% ethanol. What would be the 'proof' strength of this wine?

(c) How is the 'proof' strength of a solution found?

Summary

Fractional distillation is used to separate mixtures of miscible liquids, e.g. ethanol and water. The process depends upon the difference in boiling point of the different substances in the solution. The liquid with the lower boiling point boils off first.

The fractional distillation of liquid air (Unit 20) is another example of fractional distillation.

Unit 12

Chromatography

Chromatography is a simple method for separating a mixture of substances dissolved in a solvent. It can also be used to identify the substances.

There are many types of chromatography. The simplest is paper chromatography.

12.1 Simple paper chromatography

Ink is a mixture of dyes dissolved in water. In Unit 10 we saw that it was possible to get water from ink by distillation.

The dyes that are present in an ink can be separated by simple paper chromatography.

A spot of the ink is dropped onto the centre of a filter paper circle. The ink is left to dry. Drops of water are then dropped onto the centre of the ink spot using a teat pipette. If this is done slowly and carefully the ink blot gets larger. The different dyes present in the ink spread out at different rates. Each dye forms a separate ring.

For example, Fig. 12.1 shows the filter paper before and after adding water to the filter paper which has a blot of red ink in its centre. There are two separate red rings and the ink must be made up from two dyes.

12.2 Other ways of carrying out paper chromatography

Adding drops of water with a teat pipette needs a very steady hand. There are other ways of getting similar results.

In Fig. 12.2 there are three methods which can be used. (There are many other ways.) In **(a)** a filter paper is used which has a small 'tongue' cut out. This 'tongue' dips into the water in a beaker. The water slowly rises up the 'tongue', reaches the blot on the filter paper and spreads out as before.

In **(b)** and **(c)** the separation of dyes takes place on a strip or sheet of filter paper. In each case, the water moves upwards and the dyes separate to form spots on the filter paper. Each dye present forms a different spot. A spot or spots of the ink are placed near the bottom of the strip or sheet. This type of chromatography is called ascending chromatography and the resulting strip or sheet is called a chromatogram.

12.3 Separating colourless substances

It is easy to see the different spots or rings formed when chromatography of a coloured substance is carried out. Each dye produces a coloured ring or spot.

Solutions of colourless substances can be separated using the same methods. When you have finished, however, you will not be able to see the rings or spots which exist on the paper because they are colourless.

There are chemicals which, when sprayed on the chromatogram, make the rings or spots visible. The process is called developing. It can be compared with the process of developing in photography. The pictures exist on the film taken

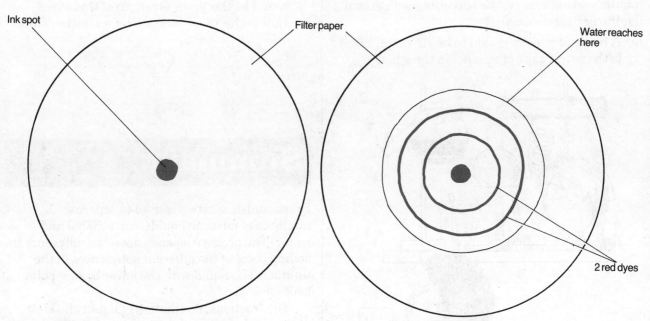

Fig. 12.1 Simple chromatography of red ink

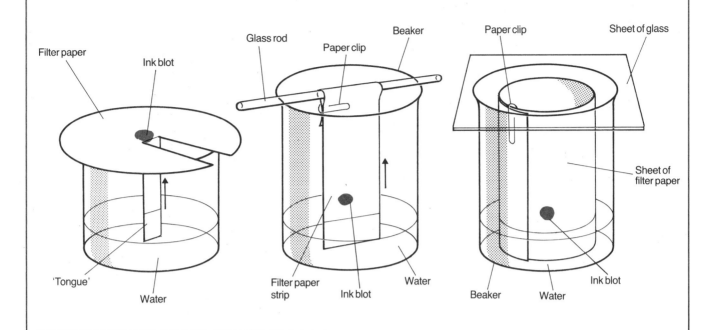

Fig. 12.2 Other chromatography methods

from the camera but you cannot see them unless chemicals are used to develop the film.

12.4 Identifying the substances present

So far we have seen that you can separate substances in solution and find out how many different substances are present. It is possible, however, actually to identify the substances present.

One way of doing this is to compare your results with the results obtained by carrying out identical experiments with known pure substances.

In Fig. 12.3 a chromatogram is shown for a blue ink. Alongside are the chromatograms obtained using pale blue, purple and dark blue

dyes under the same conditions. Before letting the chromatograms dry we must mark the final position of the solvent with a pencil. This line is called the 'solvent front'.

From the results shown in Fig. 12.3 we can conclude that:

(i) the pale blue, purple and dark blue dyes are not split up as they each produce only a single spot on the chromatogram;

(ii) the blue ink is made up from a mixture of pale blue and purple dyes. The chromatogram for the blue ink shows two spots in the same positions on the chromatogram as the spots for pale blue and purple dyes. There is no spot near the top of the chromatogram and so there is no dark blue dye present.

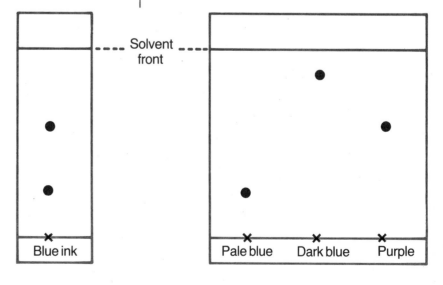

Fig. 12.3
Chromatograms obtained using
(a) blue ink and (b) pale blue,
dark blue and purple dyes

Activities

Fig. 12.4 A gas-liquid chromatograph – a most useful piece of equipment in an industrial laboratory

1   A history of chromatography.
Chromatography is a fairly simple idea but was only discovered in this century. It was first carried out in 1903 by the Russian botanist Mikhail Semenovich Tswett (1872–1919). He used a glass column packed with powdered chalk to separate plant pigments. These plant pigments were extracted by dissolving them in petrol. When this solution was poured through the column the different dyes separated and different bands formed. These bands formed because the different dyes passed through the column at different rates.

Tswett chose the word 'chromatography' which means 'colour writing'. At this time he thought his column chromatography was suitable only for separating coloured substances.

The idea of chromatography was then largely forgotten until 1931 when Kuhn and others used the method to separate vitamins. They showed that chromatography was not limited to coloured substances.

Paper chromatography, which we now take very much for granted, dates back only to 1944 when Consden, Gordon and Martin showed it to

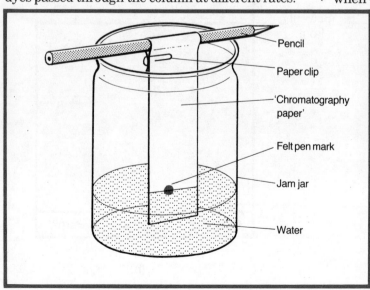

Pencil

Paper clip

'Chromatography paper'

Felt pen mark

Jam jar

Water

Fig. 12.5 Chromatography at home

be a reliable method for separating small quantities of material.

Gas-liquid chromatography is even more recent. In 1952 Martin and James showed that this method was very useful for separating tiny quantities of volatile material. A small sample is injected into a stream of carrier gas. The gases pass through a heated column. The different substances pass through at different rates.

(a) What is a botanist?

(b) How old was Tswett when he discovered chromatography?

(c) Why do you think Tswett's ideas were not followed up for nearly 30 years?

(d) Name the man who was involved in the development of both paper and gas-liquid chromatography.

(e) What was the solvent in Tswett's experiments with plant pigments?

(f) What are the advantages of paper chromatography over column chromatography?

*2 For Activities 2 and 3 you can use strips of white blotting paper or paper cut from a coffee filter bag. Cut the pieces about 3 cm wide.

In this Activity you can separate the dyes in felt pen inks. You can find the number and colour of dyes present.

Felt pen inks dissolve easily in water and can provide some interesting results. You can also use bottles of fountain pen ink but not ballpoint pen ink. This ink does not dissolve in water so the inks would not separate using water as the solvent.

Take a strip of 'chromatography' paper and draw a pencil line about 1 cm from the bottom. Using one of your felt pens, put a small ink mark on this pencil line. This mark should not be more than 3 mm diameter. Adjust the paper until it rests over a pencil and the bottom of the paper is just above the bottom of the jam jar. A paper clip will hold the paper in place. Remove the paper from the jar and put the smallest quantity of water in the bottom of the jar. Put the pencil and paper back and make sure that the paper just touches the water. Leave the jam jar undisturbed until the water has nearly reached the paper clip.

Repeat the investigation with other felt pens.

(a) What would happen if the ink blot was below the water level in the jam jar?

(b) How would you modify this experiment to make it suitable for separating ballpoint pen inks?

*3 The coloured coatings of 'Smarties' can be separated by paper chromatography. If you lick the edge of a 'Smartie' you can rub a small coloured mark onto the 'chromatography' paper. You can repeat the process in Activity 2.

4 A forensic scientist is a person who can solve crimes by using science. Explain how a forensic scientist could find out which one of two different coloured felt pens was used to write a 'poison-pen' letter.

5 A public analyst is employed by a local council to carry out a whole series of scientific tests for our safety.

There are only a limited number of artificial food dyes which can be used to colour certain types of food.

It is believed that a certain brand of orange squash being sold by supermarkets contains a dye which is not allowed.

The public analyst takes a sample of this squash and, by clever Chemistry, manages to get a sample of the orange colouring.

Explain how the public analyst would show:

(a) that the orange colouring consists of a mixture of two dyes;

(b) that one of these dyes is illegal.

6 The green colour in grass is due to the presence of two dyes – a green dye called chlorophyll and a yellow dye called xanthophyll. These dyes do not dissolve in water but dissolve in a solvent called propanone.

(a) Explain how you would get a solution of the dyes from grass.

(b) A drop of this dye solution was put in the centre of a filter paper.

(i) Which solvent should be added to the filter paper to make the blot bigger and spread out the dyes?

(ii) Draw a diagram of the chromatogram, labelling the green and yellow dyes. (Chlorophyll does not spread out as much as xanthophyll.)

(c) When extracting the green colour from grass using propanone, the best results are obtained when propanone is heated to about 60°C. Propanone is, however, highly flammable.

Draw a diagram to show how a test tube containing propanone could be heated without risk of the propanone catching fire.

Summary

Chromatography is a method of separating a mixture of substances in solution. There are different types of chromatography including column chromatography, paper chromatography, and gas-liquid chromatography.

Unit 13

Sublimation

Most solid substances, when heated, will melt and form a liquid. On further heating the liquid boils and forms a gas. The reverse occurs on cooling.

This can be summarized as follows:

Solid ⇌ Liquid ⇌ Gas

There are a few substances which do not do this and miss out the liquid stage.

13.1 Sublimation

Ammonium chloride is a white solid at room temperature. When it is heated in a dry test tube the solid turns straight to a gas. It does not melt. The amount of solid in the bottom of the test tube decreases and eventually the solid will disappear completely from the bottom of the test tube.

As the gas formed passes up the test tube it cools. It reforms the white solid on the cool glass at the top of the test tube. The solid formed is still ammonium chloride. The chemical is unchanged but has moved up the test tube. This is summarized in Fig. 13.1.

The change from solid straight to gas is called **vaporization**. The reverse process where a gas turns directly to a solid on cooling is called **sublimation**.

13.2 Other substances which sublime

There are only a few substances which behave in this way. Ammonium chloride is most commonly quoted as an example. Ammonium carbonate behaves in a very similar way.

Iodine is a grey-black shiny solid. On heating it melts and forms a dark-coloured liquid. Soon after melting it forms a purple gas. Solid iodine crystals reform on the cooler part of the test tube. Iodine is said to sublime because the iodine gas turns directly to a solid on cooling.

13.3 Separating a mixture of ammonium chloride and sodium chloride

A mixture of ammonium chloride and sodium chloride cannot be separated in the same way as a mixture of sand and salt. Both substances dissolve in water. They can be separated, however, using the knowledge that ammonium chloride sublimes. The apparatus in Fig. 13.2 is suitable for this.

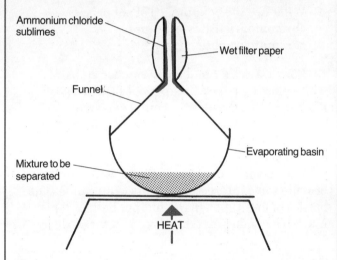

Fig. 13.2 Separating a mixture containing ammonium chloride

The mixture to be separated is placed in the evaporating basin and the evaporating basin is heated gently with a Bunsen burner. Ammonium chloride vaporizes and sublimes. It collects inside the funnel. The sodium chloride does not vaporize and remains in the evaporating basin. The wet filter papers keep the funnel cool.

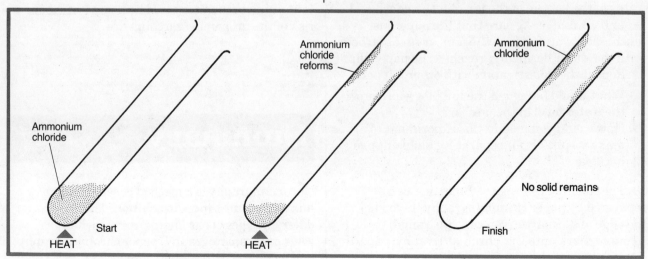

Fig. 13.1 Heating ammonium chloride

Activities

*1 A torch battery (e.g. HP2) contains ammonium chloride. In this activity you can separate some ammonium chloride from the battery using sublimation. Carefully cut open a spent battery with a hacksaw. Do not use a transistor radio battery (e.g. PP9). Inside the battery you will find a black paste and a black solid carbon rod. Save the carbon rod. It will be useful in later activities! Put some of the black paste into a test tube and push it to the bottom. Heat the test tube gently. White crystals of ammonium chloride will collect on the cooler part of the test tube.

*2 A toilet deodorant block contains the chemical paradichlorobenzene. This substance sublimes and you can produce a very startling example of sublimation. Put a toilet deodorant block into a dry glass bottle with a screw top. Place this bottle in a warm place for a couple of weeks. The paradichlorobenzene vaporizes and sublimes on the cooler glass. Some very impressive crystals of paradichlorobenzene will be formed (see Fig. 13.3).

3 A chemical fertilizer contains a mixture of three substances: ammonium chloride, urea and potassium chloride. The properties of these three substances are summarized in Table 13.1.

Substance	State at room temperature	Solubility in water	Change on heating
Ammonium chloride	Solid	Dissolves well	Sublimes
Urea	Solid	Does not dissolve	Melts
Potassium chloride	Solid	Dissolves well	Melts

Table 13.1 The constituents of a fertilizer and their properties

Describe clearly how you would get some pure samples of each chemical from the mixture in the fertilizer.

Summary

Sublimation is a useful method for separating mixtures containing a component which readily vaporizes on heating. On cooling, the gas formed reforms the original solid substance. This process is called sublimation.

Ammonium chloride and iodine are the usual examples given for sublimation.

Fig. 13.3 Crystals of paradichlorobenzene formed by sublimation

Unit 14

Pure substances

In Units 9–13 methods for purifying chemicals were explained. These included:

filtration;
centrifuging;
decanting;
evaporation;
distillation;
fractional distillation;
chromatography;
sublimation.

Pure substances are often difficult to produce and, as a result, expensive to buy. In chemical experiments we usually use pure substances.

14.1 Recognizing a pure substance

A pure substance contains only the named chemical. It does not contain other substances called **impurities**.

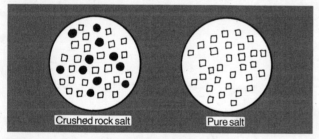

Fig. 14.1 Rock salt and pure salt viewed through a hand lens

It is often difficult to tell from looking whether a substance is pure or not. A lump of rock salt is obviously not pure. When crushed and viewed through a hand lens, dark pieces can be seen (Fig. 14.1).

The best simple tests of purity that can be used are melting (or freezing) point and boiling point. A pure substance always has a sharp melting and boiling point. For example, pure liquid water boils at 100°C (at normal pressure).

Solid ice melts at 0°C.

If the water is not pure (i.e. it is impure because other substances are present) the boiling point is slightly higher (perhaps 103°C). If ice contains impurities the melting point will be below 0°C and the melting will take place over a range of temperature (perhaps −2 to −3°C).

If you wish to find out if a substance is pure you should carry out simple tests to find the melting and/or boiling point of the substance. Suitable tests are shown in Fig. 14.2.
N.B. In both cases the thermometer is in the liquid being tested. In (b) the liquid should be stirred continuously.

14.2 Grades of purity

When buying chemicals to use there are different qualities which can be bought.

Technical grade (or Tech.) is a low-priced form of the chemical where purity is not important. For example, if salt was required to make a cooling bath for the investigation in Fig. 14.2(b), technical grade would be suitable.

Laboratory grade (or L.R.) is the usual grade of chemical for laboratory use. The amount of impurities is less than in technical grade and the maximum levels of impurity are known.

Analytical grade (or A.R.) is for chemicals of the highest purity used for special purposes.

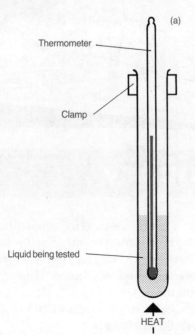

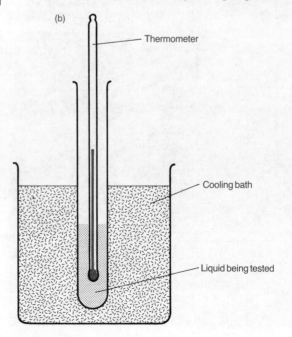

Fig. 14.2 Finding (a) the boiling point and (b) the melting (freezing) point

Activities

Calcium metal, granules

25 g	£2.75
100 g	£4.25
250 g	£7.50

Ca

Contact with water liberates highly flammable gas

Calcium carbonate, LR (powder)

1 kg	£2.16
3 kg	£4.40

$CaCO_3$
Assay, min. 98.5% (on dried)
Maximum limits of impurities

Acid insoluble	0.05%
Arsenic (As)	0.0004%
Chloride (Cl)	0.05%
Iron (Fe)	0.02%
Lead (Pb)	0.002%
Loss on drying (105°C)	1%
Sulphate (SO_4)	0.25%

Calcium carbonate, AR (powder)

250 g	£4.60
500 g	£7.05

$CaCO_3$
Assay, min. 99.5%

Ammonia (NH_3)	<0.1%
Barium and strontium (Ba)	<0.04%
Chloride (Cl)	<0.001%
Heavy metals (Pb)	<0.001%
Iron (Fe)	<0.001%
Magnesium (Mg)	<0.01%
Nitrate (NO_3)	<0.01%
Phosphate (PO_4)	<0.001%
Potassium (K)	<0.01%
Silicate (SiO_2)	<0.01%
Sodium (Na)	<0.02%
Soluble alkali	<0.25 milli equivs %
Sulphate (SO_4)	<0.005%

Calcium carbonate, Iceland spar

25 g	£2.85

Calcium carbonate (Marble chippings)
approx. 13mm (irregular) (Calcium carbonate ore)

1 kg	£2.06
3 kg	£3.70

Calcium chloride LR, hexahydrate (crystals)

500 g	£3.61

$CaCl_2.6H_2O$
Assay, min. 98%
Maximum limits of impurities

Aluminium, iron and acid insoluble	0.2%
Arsenic (As)	0.0002%
Free acid (HCl)	0.01%
Free alkali ($Ca(OH)_2$)	0.01%
Lead (Pb)	0.025%
Sulphate (SO_4)	0.025%

Low melting point substance

Calcium hydroxide, LR (powder)

1 kg	£3.33

$Ca(OH)_2$
Assay, min. 90%
Maximum limits of impurities

Aluminium, iron and acid insoluble	1%
Arsenic (As)	0.0005%
Chloride (Cl)	0.05%
Lead (Pb)	0.005%
Sulphate (SO_4)	0.5%

Calcium oxide, Technical, lump (Quicklime)

1 kg	£3.46
3 kg	£4.46

Causes burns

Table 14.1 Part of a chemical catalogue

1 Table 14.1 shows part of a chemical catalogue. Use this information to answer the following questions:

(a) What is the meaning of the word 'assay'?

(b) How should calcium be stored safely?

(c) What is the advantage and what is the disadvantage of buying calcium in large quantities?

(d) Name two natural forms of calcium carbonate mentioned in the catalogue.

(e) Name one chemical sold in
  (i) technical grade;
  (ii) laboratory reagent grade;
  (iii) analytical reagent grade.

(f) Why is it unlikely that calcium chloride hexahydrate is made from calcium granules?

2 During a laboratory investigation too much chemical was taken from the bottle. At the end of the investigation, John was about to return unused chemical to the bottle when the teacher stopped him. Why is it unwise to returned unused chemical to the bottle?

Summary

A pure chemical contains no impurities. It has a sharp melting and boiling point.

Unit 15

Chemicals

Where they come from

A *wide range of chemicals is used during a Chemistry course. At this stage it is interesting to consider where chemicals come from. Few chemicals are found in a pure state. A great deal of purification is required to get the level of purity essential for use in the laboratory.*

15.1 Chemicals from the earth

The rocks of the earth are a major source of a wide range of the raw materials for the chemical industry.

Fig. 15.1 shows a pie diagram giving the composition of the rocks of the earth.

Most of the rocks are composed largely of oxygen, silicon and aluminium. Metals which we

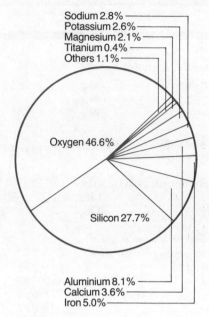

Sodium 2.8%
Potassium 2.6%
Magnesium 2.1%
Titanium 0.4%
Others 1.1%

Oxygen 46.6%

Silicon 27.7%

Aluminium 8.1%
Calcium 3.6%
Iron 5.0%

Fig. 15.1 Composition of rocks of the earth

use in large quantities are only present in small amounts in the earth.

E.g. Copper   0.007%
       Silver   0.00001%
       Gold   0.0000005%

Gold was the first metal to be obtained from the earth. This is almost certainly because it can be found in a metallic form in the earth as small flakes or nuggets and does not need extracting. The Egyptians established a gold working industry over 4000 years ago.

Mineral	Chemical composition	Origin	Uses
Salt	Sodium chloride	Evaporation of inland salty lakes	Making chlorine, bleaches, pottery glazes, sodium carbonate (washing soda) Flavouring and preserving food
Marble Limestone Chalk	Calcium carbonate	Shells of dead sea animals	Making lime (calcium hydroxide), cement (roasting limestone with sand and aluminium oxide), glass (heating limestone with sand and sodium carbonate)
Coal	Largely carbon	Effect of pressure and temperature on trees and plants over millions of years	Fuel and source of carbon chemicals
Oil and natural gas	Largely a mixture of hydrocarbons	Effect of pressure and temperature on animal and vegetable material over millions of years	Fuel and source of carbon chemicals
Sulphur	Sulphur	Decomposition of calcium sulphate – volcanic gases	Making sulphuric acid. Vulcanizing (hardening) rubber

Table 15.1 Important minerals in the earth

Other metals exist in the earth in **ores**. The ore has to be chemically treated to produce the pure metal (Volume 2).

The earth also provides other chemicals in large quantities. These include salt (sodium chloride), sulphur and limestone. These are used in large quantities in the chemical industry.

The earth also provides *fossil fuels*, including coal, crude oil and natural gas.

Table 15.1 summarizes some of the uses of these important minerals.

15.2 Chemicals from the sea

Soluble substances from the rocks of the earth are washed into the sea by rivers. Since three quarters of the earth's surface is covered by sea, there are tremendous possibilities for obtaining chemicals from sea water.

Fig. 15.2 shows the composition of a typical sample of sea water. Many substances are present in sea water in tiny amounts. Sodium chloride (salt) is obviously obtained from sea water. Magnesium and bromine are extracted economically from sea water.

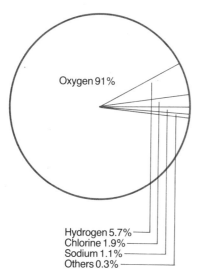

Oxygen 91%
Hydrogen 5.7%
Chlorine 1.9%
Sodium 1.1%
Others 0.3%

Fig. 15.2 Composition of sea water

It has been estimated that one cubic mile of sea water contains £100 000 000 worth of gold dissolved in it. It is, however, impossible to extract it economically at present because the gold is mixed with 150 000 000 tonnes of other dissolved substances.

Sea water is a source of the chemical family called the **halogens**. The uses of the halogens are summarized in Table 15.2.

The sea bed is a largely untapped source of metals. Lumps, called nodules, on the sea bed contain a wide range of metals. Recovering them is expensive but worthwhile.

15.3 Chemicals from the air

The air provides a wide range of gases including oxygen, nitrogen, argon and neon. These gases can be obtained by fractional distillation of liquid air (Unit 11).

15.4 Chemicals from plants

Trees, plants and vegetables provide a wide range of chemicals. Vegetable fats and oils are valuable chemical raw materials used in the manufacture of margarine and soap.

Other substances such as sugars and starch can be extracted from plant material.

Halogen	Amount dissolved in 1 cubic mile of sea water	Uses
Fluorine	7000 tonnes	Fluorides are added to tap water and toothpaste to reduce tooth decay
Chlorine	100 000 000 tonnes	As a bleaching and germ-killing agent; for making a wide range of chlorine compounds including plastics (PVC) and insecticides (DDT)
Bromine	300 000 tonnes	For making dibromoethane (a petrol additive); BCF for fire extinguishers; bleaching and germ-killing
Iodine	250 tonnes	Solution of iodine in ethanol used as an antiseptic. For making quartz-iodine bulbs

Table 15.2 The uses of the halogens

Activities

1 Fig. 15.3 shows limestone being quarried and a factory which turns limestone into cement. Limestone quarrying can spoil a landscape and the industry can cause problems in a rural area.

What can be done to restore the land after quarrying?

What other problems could this industry cause?

What advantages could it bring to the area?

2 The world's scarce resources can be preserved by re-cycling.

(a) What is re-cycling?

(b) Which materials are re-cycled at present?

The following account outlines a new process for extracting valuable metal from household rubbish. Read the account and answer the questions which follow.

Fig. 15.3 Limestone quarrying and cement making

THE SUNDAY TIMES

SCRAP METAL worth £4½ million is being buried every year on rubbish dumps around Britain. Now a new process developed at the Government-financed Warren Spring technology laboratory at Stevenage, Herts, makes it possible to reclaim almost all of it.

About 1 million tonnes of old cars, cookers, fridges, washing machines and other scrap metal are thrown out every year in the UK and find their way to the scrap merchants' yards where they are smashed up. The iron and steel which represents three-quarters of the scrap is picked out with magnets.

Nine-tenths of the rest consists of glass, wood, rubber, plastics and textiles. But the other 10% is a mix of valuable non-ferrous metals – brass, copper, aluminium and so on. At present these metals are retrieved by hand – a very wasteful procedure which, research has shown, only recovers about 40% of the metals. The other 60%, about 15 000 tonnes a year with a minimum value of £300 per tonne, is thrown away.

The team at Warren Spring, led by Maurice Webb and Ray New, devised a system using a vibrator to arrange the lumps of scrap metal in a neat evenly-spaced row along a conveyor and then scanning them one by one with X-rays. Different metals re-emit X-rays at different frequencies, so the team programmed a microprocessor to identify up to 14 metals and to activate swinging arms or blasts of air to sort them out.

The system sorts five lumps of metal a second, 25 times faster than any rival. Besides scrap merchants, potential customers include mining concerns who could use multi-channel systems of huge capacity to pick out metal-rich lumps of ore for crushing, steel makers who want to avoid remelting scrap with high levels of impurities in it and dealers in scrap aircraft.

John Newell
The Sunday Times (8 July 1984)

(c) How can the iron and steel be removed?
(d) Name three non-ferrous metals.
(e) Give two advantages of this process over the method in use at present.
(f) How would you attempt to show that hand picking only removes 40% of the non-ferrous metals?

3 It might one day be possible to obtain valuable minerals from the moon or from other planets. At present the costs would be too high to consider it.

The American Apollo missions and the Russian Luna unmanned expeditions have shown that some of the rocks on the moon are older than the rocks on the Earth. Table 15.3 gives the composition of the rocks of the moon.

Activities continued

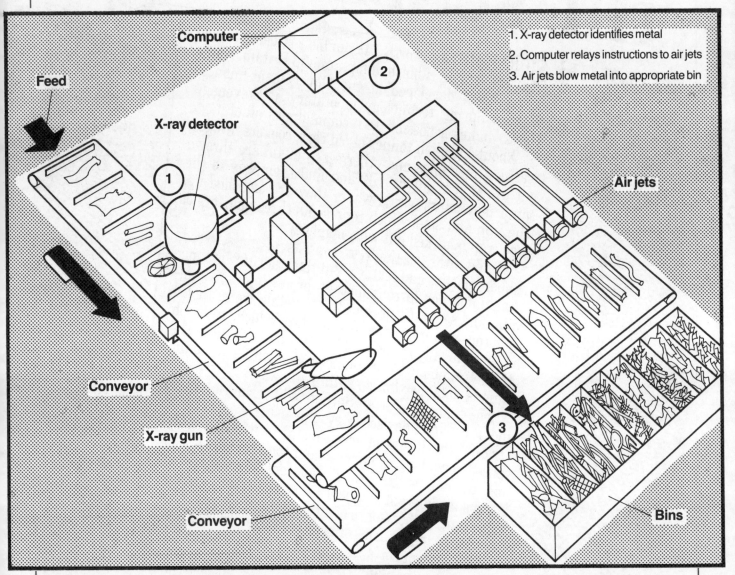

Feed

Computer

X-ray detector

1. X-ray detector identifies metal

2. Computer relays instructions to air jets

3. Air jets blow metal into appropriate bin

Air jets

Conveyor

X-ray gun

Conveyor

Bins

Fig. 15.4 A new way of extracting metals from household rubbish

Substance	Percentage by mass
Oxygen	43
Silicon	21
Aluminium	7
Magnesium	5
Calcium	9
Iron	12
Titanium	2
Sodium	0.5
Others	0.5

Table 15.3 Composition of the moon

Draw a pie diagram (like Fig. 15.1) to show the composition of the moon.

Write a short paragraph to compare the composition of the earth and the moon.

4 Fig. 15.5 shows rock salt being mined from underground deposits in Cheshire.

(a) Much of the salt is used as salt solution (called brine). Suggest an alternative way of getting salt as brine from underground deposits. Why is this method not suitable for getting limestone?

(b) Maps of Cheshire drawn in the 17th century do not show inland lakes called 'meres' which exist today. They seem to have appeared in the past 300 years. Explain why these lakes appeared.

Fig. 15.5 Common salt (sodium chloride) is mined in Britain as rock salt. Here it is being loaded at the working face of the Meadow Bank Mine

5 Which of the three factors below would affect the cost of a particular metal?

(i) The demand for the metal by customers.

(ii) The amount of metal ore in the earth.

(iii) The difficulty of extracting the metal from the ore.

6 The tin mines in Cornwall were largely abandoned because rich deposits of tin ore were found in Malaysia. List three changes which could revive interest in re-opening the Cornish tin mines.

Summary

Chemicals come from a wide range of places. The rocks of the earth are the most important source. We are becoming aware that the resources are limited and they must be used with care or they will be exhausted. More effort will have to be made to find alternative sources of energy to replace fossil fuels and, in particular, to re-cycle metals.

Few chemicals are obtained in a pure state and expensive processing is necessary to get the necessary purity.

Unit 16

Acids and alkalis

Many of the everyday substances we use at home are acids. The 'opposite' of an acid is an alkali. In this unit we are going to look at some of the properties of acids and alkalis and how they can be detected.

16.1 Acids

Many substances, e.g. vinegar, lemon juice and apples, contain acids. Acids always have a sour taste but often you would be unwise to try to taste them!

In the laboratory there are three common acids called mineral acids. They are called

sulphuric acid
nitric acid
hydrochloric acid

16.2 Alkalis

Alkalis are also commonly found at home. They include baking powder, washing soda, ammonia solution and oven cleaners. They all have a soapy feel when touched.

Common alkalis in the laboratory include

sodium hydroxide (previously called caustic soda)

potassium hydroxide (caustic potash)

calcium hydroxide (limewater)

The word 'alkali' comes from the Arabic word for ashes. Alkalis were first obtained from the ashes of plant and animal fires. The word 'caustic' means burning and suggests the corrosive properties of alkalis.

16.3 Neutral substances

A substance which is neither an acid nor an alkali is said to be **neutral**. Pure water, salt solution and petrol are neutral.

16.4 Detecting acids and alkalis

The simplest way of detecting an acid or an alkali is to use an **indicator**. An indicator is a plant dye in solution which changes colour depending upon whether it is in an acid or an alkali. By its colour it indicates the presence of an acid or an alkali.

A wide variety of plant dyes can be used (see Activities). In the laboratory we usually use a solution of litmus. This is made from a type of lichen which grows in cold lands near the North Pole. When added to an acid it turns red and when added to an alkali it turns blue.

Remember   **red** in acid
            blue in alkali

In neutral solutions it is purple but this is sometimes difficult to see.

Litmus can either be used as a solution or, soaked into pieces of paper and dried, as litmus paper.

It will detect an acid or an alkali but it cannot indicate how strong an acid or alkali is.

16.5 pH

The pH scale is a scale which shows how strong or weak an acid or alkali is. It is a scale from 1 to 14. A substance which is an acid has a pH less than 7. One which is an alkali has a pH greater than 7. A neutral substance has a pH of exactly 7.

The pH of a solution can be found in two ways.

(i) Using universal indicator
Universal indicator is a mixture of simple indicators. Instead of changing colour just once it changes colour a number of times.

Fig. 16.1 Universal indicator paper in different forms

	pH	Colour of universal indicator	Examples in the home	Examples in the laboratory
STRONG ACIDS	1	Red	Car battery acid	Mineral acids
	2			
	3			
	4		Lemon juice, vinegar	Ethanoic acid
WEAK ACIDS	5	Orange		
	6	Yellow	Soda water	Carbonic acid
NEUTRAL	7	Green	Water, salt	
	8	Blue	Soap, baking powder	Sodium hydrogen carbonate
	9	Indigo	Indigestion tablets	
WEAK ALKALIS	10	Purple		Ammonia solution
	11		Washing soda	
	12		Oven cleaner	
	13			
STRONG ALKALIS	14			Sodium and potassium hydroxides

Table 16.1 The pH scale

In Table 16.1 the different colours for simple universal indicator are given. If a couple of drops of universal indicator are added to a solution and the indicator turns blue the solution has a pH of 8 and is therefore a very weak alkali.

There are different types of universal indicator with different colour changes. It is therefore possible, for example, to distinguish pH values of 1,2,3 and 4.

Paper soaked in universal indicator solution and dried is often more convenient to use. This paper is called either universal indicator paper or pH paper.

(ii) Using a pH meter

A pH meter is an electrical device widely used in industrial laboratories to measure pH accurately. A glass probe is put into the solution being tested and the pH can be read from a dial or a digital read-out immediately.

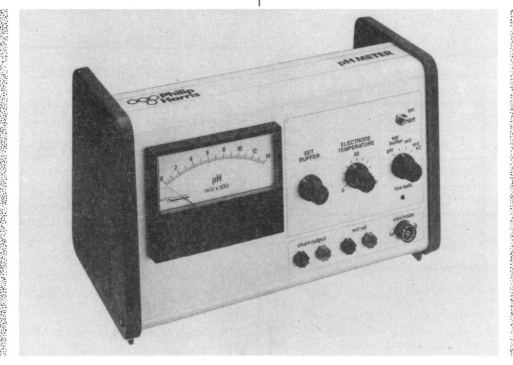

Fig. 16.2 A pH meter

Activities

*1 Using plant dyes to detect acids and alkalis.

Cut up pieces of raw beetroot into small shreds with a knife. Put these shreds into a test tube and add just enough water to cover them. Heat the test tube gently until the water starts to boil. You can use a strip of paper wrapped round the neck of the test tube to hold it during heating (Fig. 16.3). Carefully decant the solution into another test tube. Most of the dye from the beetroot has dissolved in the water and formed a plant **extract**.

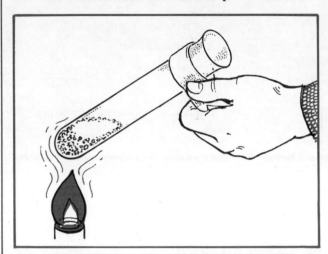

Fig. 16.3 Making a plant dye to use in detecting acids and alkalis

Put a couple of drops of this beetroot extract into two clean test tubes. Add lemon juice (an acid) to the extract in the first test tube. Add some washing soda solution (an alkali) to the extract in the second tube. The solutions in the two test tubes should be different colours as the beetroot extract is a good indicator. Record the colours in Table 16.2.

Plant dye	Colour in acid solution	Colour in alkali solution
Litmus	Red	Blue
Red cabbage		

Table 16.2 Plant dyes as indicators

Having successfully carried out this activity with beetroot you can try other plant materials. Red cabbage is very suitable and can be obtained throughout the year. Blackcurrant and blackberry juices also work well. Flowers also provide good results, especially rose, dahlia, tulip and carnation petals. Avoid yellow flowers such as daffodils and dandelions which do not work. You can record the results of these investigations in Table 16.2.

You can then use the plant dye extracts to test household substances to see if they are acid or alkali.

Why is it impossible to use plant dyes to test whether tomato sauce is an acid or an alkali?

*2 You may be able to buy strips of litmus paper and universal indicator paper. They are readily available as spares for Chemistry sets and in some good chemist's shops. Universal indicator paper may also be available at a good garden shop where it is sold for testing the soil.

If you can get hold of these you can safely test a wide range of household substances. With litmus paper you can test to see if a substance is acid or alkali. With universal indicator you can find the pH of the substance. You can then produce a chart like the one in Fig. 16.4.

	Acid		Neutral		Alkaline	
Substance	pH 1 2 3	4 5 6	7	8 9	10 11	12 13
Vinegar		✗				
Washing soda						✗
Baking powder					✗	
Salt				✗		
Toothpaste			✗			
Lemon juice	✗					
Domestos						✗
Liver salts	✗					
Bicarbonate of soda				✗		

Fig. 16.4 A pH chart for common household substances

The indicator must be dipped in water before use and then pressed against the substance if it is a solid.

3 Table 16.3 gives the colour of four different indicators in solutions of different pH. The gap in each case between colours corresponds to the pH at which the indicator changes colour.

(a) What colour is a solution of pH 8 with a couple of drops of bromocresol green indicator added?

(b) A solution turns yellow when either methol orange or phenol red is added. What is the approximate pH of the solution?

(c) A mixture of methyl orange, bromocresol green and phenolphthalein is added to pure water

Indicator	pH	1	2	3	4	5	6	7	8	9	10	11	12	13	14
Methyl orange		← Red →			←				Yellow						→
Bromocresol green		← Yellow →			←				Blue						→
Phenol red		← Yellow →						←			Red				→
Phenolphthalein		← Colourless →						←			Red				→

Table 16.3 The colours of indicators in solutions of different pH

(pH 7). What is the colour of the resulting solution?

4 The colours of simple universal indicator are: red, orange, yellow, green, blue, indigo, violet. Where in nature is this order of colours found?

5 Five test tubes labelled **A**, **B**, **C**, **D** and **E** contain five different liquids. These liquids are: water, hydrochloric acid, sodium hydroxide solution, salt solution, ethanoic acid. It is not known which liquid is in which test tube.

The liquids were tested with
   (i) litmus;
   (ii) universal indicator.
These results are shown in Table 16.4.

Liquid	Colour with litmus	Colour with universal indicator	pH
A	Red	Red	1
B	Blue	Purple	13
C	Purple	Green	
D	Red	Orange	
E	Purple		7

Table 16.4 Tests to distinguish between five different liquids

(a) Complete Table 16.4.

(b) Which test tube contains
   (i) hydrochloric acid?
   (ii) ethanoic acid?
   (iii) sodium hydroxide solution?

(c) Which test tubes contain either water or salt solution?

(d) How, apart from taste, could you find out which test tube contained water and which contained salt solution?

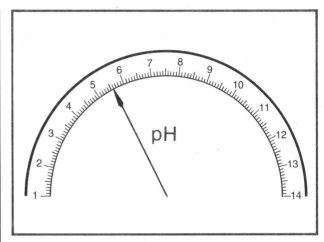

Fig. 16.5 A dial recording the pH of a solution

6 Fig. 16.5 shows a dial recording the pH of a solution labelled **X**.
   (i) What is the pH of the solution labelled **X**?
   (ii) What can be concluded about this solution from the pH?
   (iii) Which one of the following substances would, when added to **X**, produce a solution with a pH of 2?

   water, universal indicator, hydrochloric acid, ethanoic acid, sodium hydroxide

Summary

An acid is a substance with a sour taste. It turns the indicator called litmus red. The common acids are sulphuric acid, hydrochloric acid and nitric acid.

The 'opposite' of an acid is an alkali. Alkalis have a soapy feel and turn litmus blue.

A substance which is neither acid nor alkali is said to be neutral.

The pH of a substance is a measure of how acid or alkaline a substance is. The pH can be found using a mixture of indicators called universal indicator.

Unit 17

Neutralization

Acids have a pH less than 7 and alkalis have a pH greater than 7. If an acid and an alkali are mixed together in the correct amounts a neutral solution is produced. A reaction of this type is called a **neutralization** reaction.

17.1 Using acids and alkalis safely

Acids and alkalis must always be used with great care. Goggles must always be worn as both can cause nasty burns and other injuries.

If an acid is split in the laboratory it should be neutralized by adding bicarbonate of soda (sodium hydrogen carbonate – a weak alkali). Only when the acid is neutralized should the spill be wiped up, using a wet cloth and plenty of water.

Similarly, a strong alkali should be treated with a weak acid (e.g. ethanoic acid – vinegar) before wiping up.

17.2 Acids in digestion

Your stomach contains over 1000 cm^3 of hydrochloric acid. This acid does you no harm. In fact you need it to create the right conditions for digesting your food. During digestion your food is broken down into simpler substances which can be used by your body. These are the vital supplies that your body needs for all kinds of jobs including building, repair and providing energy.

From time to time you might suffer pain due to indigestion. This is caused by too much acid, i.e. excess acidity. You can cure indigestion by taking antacids such as bicarbonate of soda (sodium hydrogen carbonate). These substances are weak alkalis and neutralize excess acid. It is wise to see your doctor if the indigestion keeps on coming back in case there is some other problem.

17.3 Soil testing

Soil with a pH of between 6.5 and 7 is the most suitable for growing a wide range of plants. If the pH value drops below 6 the soil becomes too acid. If it rises above 8 it becomes too alkaline. In either case it will not give good results.

Soil varies greatly from place to place. It is important to know the pH of your soil and how the pH can be controlled.

Excess acidity in soil is the most important cause of crop failure. If we always kept the pH of soil in mind we could improve the food production of the world by 20%.

Excess acidity is caused by rainwater (which is itself slightly acid) constantly washing alkali from the soil. This causes 'soil sourness'. The excess acidity can be neutralized by adding lime (calcium hydroxide).

Using certain fertilizers such as ammonium sulphate might make plants grow better but they often make the soil more acid.

17.4 Insect bites and stings

We have all felt the discomfort of insect bites and stings. These involve the injection of a small amount of chemical into the skin which causes irritation.

Bee stings involve the injection of acid into the skin and should be treated with calamine lotion (a suspension of zinc carbonate) or bicarbonate of soda. These are weak alkalis. They neutralize the acid and reduce the irritation. (Bees sometimes leave part of their sting in the skin and this should be carefully wiped out.)

Wasp stings, however, are different as they involve an alkali being injected into the skin. The poison should be neutralized by treating with vinegar (a weak acid).

Fig. 17.1 Neutralization

Activities

*1 You can easily demonstrate neutralization in your mouth and enjoy it! You can buy acid drop sweets in a good sweet shop. Put one of these sweets in your mouth and suck it for a short while. You will soon recognize a sour taste. This is caused by the presence of the weak acid, citric acid, in the sweet.

Put some bicarbonate of soda (from a chemist) on the palm of your hand and lick it from your hand with your tongue. You will soon notice that the sour taste has gone. The citric acid has been neutralized by the weak alkali.

*2 Put a small volume of vinegar into a test tube and add some bicarbonate of soda powder. Observe carefully what happens in this neutralization. You will meet this reaction in Activity 3.

*3 Making golden honeycomb
Ingredients:
200 g granulated sugar
5 fluid ounces (120 cm^3) water
small knob of butter
2 tablespoonfuls (20 cm^3) vinegar
¼ teaspoonful (1 g) bicarbonate of soda
Dissolve the sugar in the mixture of water and butter in a large, heavy-based saucepan. Do not use your mother's best saucepan!

Bring the mixture to the boil and boil until it reaches about 140°C (it does not matter if you have no kitchen thermometer as accurate temperature measurement is unimportant). Stir in the vinegar and bicarbonate of soda. The toffee produced will rise immediately so make sure it does not spill. Pour the mixture into a greased tin. When it is cool cut or break it into pieces.

4 Elaine suggested that a 'stinging nettle' plant contains an acid which is injected into the skin of the unfortunate victim.

Explain how she could show that a 'stinging nettle' contained an acid. Give the apparatus and chemicals she should use and explain the steps she should follow.

When stung by a 'stinging nettle' one can get immediate relief by rubbing the sting with the leaf of a 'dock' plant which grows close by. If the 'stinging nettle' contains an acid, suggest what might be present in a 'dock' leaf and explain why it helps.

5 Look in a gardening book and find out which plants, trees and shrubs like acid soils and which like alkaline soils. If you look at plants which grow well in your neighbourhood you might be able to guess whether your soil is acid or alkaline.

6 Robin spilt his Indian meal from the 'take-away' onto a clean white cotton teeshirt.

When the shirt was washed in cold water the stain remained. When the stain was rubbed with soap the stain changed colour from yellow to pink. The stain then washed out with cold water.

(a) Soap contains an alkali. Why does the stain change colour and what is the soap doing?
(b) What would have happened if vinegar had been poured onto the teeshirt after rubbing with soap?
(c) Suggest one other way of removing this stain.

7 Fig. 17.2 shows a simple crossword. Many of the missing words will be found in Units 16 and 17.

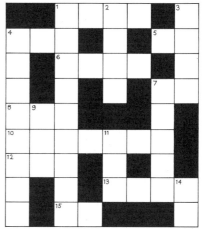

Fig. 17.2 Try this puzzle when you have read Units 16 and 17

Across
1. Bicarbonate of _____ is a weak alkali.
4. A flightless bird.
5. An electrical abbreviation.
6. An alkali in the garden.
7. An abbreviation for a doctor.
8. Left after a fire.
10. pH 7
11. Used to row a boat.
13. Cure for a sting!
15. A metal (abbreviation).

Down
1. The acid in a car battery.
2. Indicator paper should be _____ before use.
3. Neutralizes an alkali.
4. The acid in vinegar.
7. The acid in apples.
9. An expanse of water.
11. Colour of litmus in acid.
14. Abbreviation for a rare gas.

Summary

Neutralization is an important process in Chemistry. It involves the reaction of an acid with an alkali to form a neutral product.

Unit 18

Collecting gases

In this unit we are going to look at methods of handling and collecting gases. The method used for a particular gas depends upon the properties of the gas. There are five methods of collecting gases:

(i) in a gas syringe;
(ii) over water;
(iii) by downward delivery;
(iv) by upward delivery;
(v) by liquefying the gas.

18.1 Collecting in a gas syringe

This method is useful for collecting a small volume of a gas (up to 100 cm^3) and measuring its volume. It can be used for any gas. It is important to make sure that the gas syringe is connected to the gas supply without any leak.

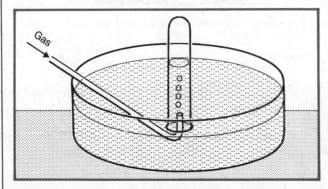

Fig. 18.1 Collecting a gas over water

18.2 Collecting a gas over water (*Fig. 18.1*)

This method can only be used to collect a gas which does not dissolve well in water, for example, oxygen. It cannot, therefore, be used to collect hydrogen chloride or ammonia. It also cannot be used to collect a dry gas.

As the gas is collected the water in the tube is replaced. It is easy to see when the test tube is full of gas.

If the gas is required dry it can be collected in a similar way but using mercury as the liquid instead of water. This is, however, very expensive because mercury is very expensive.

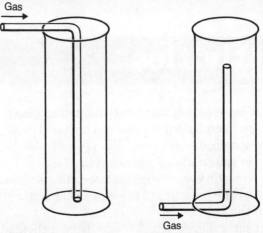

Fig. 18.2 Collecting a gas by downward delivery

Fig. 18.3 Collecting a gas by upward delivery

18.3 Collecting a gas by downward delivery (*Fig. 18.2*)

This method can be used to collect a gas which is denser than air. The gas collects at the bottom of the gas jar and pushes out the air. It is impossible to see when the gas fills the gas jar if the gas is colourless.

This method can be used for gases such as sulphur dioxide and carbon dioxide. The method is sometimes called upward displacement of air. It can be used to collect a dry gas.

18.4 Collecting a gas by upward delivery (*Fig. 18.3*)

This is suitable for collecting a gas which is less dense than air. This time the air is pushed out downwards as the gas collects. The method is sometimes called downward displacement of air. It is suitable for collecting gases such as hydrogen and ammonia.

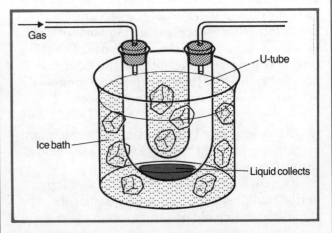

Fig. 18.4 Collecting a gas by liquefaction

18.5 Collecting a gas by liquefying (*Fig. 18.4*)

This method can only be used if the gas readily turns to a liquid on cooling. The gas is passed through a U-shaped tube dipped into a suitable ice bath. The gas turns to a liquid and collects at the bottom of the U-tube.

It can be used to collect steam and nitrogen dioxide, for example.

Activities

1 The diagrams showing methods of collecting gases are all drawn in three dimensions. Draw each of these as section diagrams (see Unit 7).

2 Ammonia is a gas which can be collected by upward delivery because it is less dense than air. It turns red litmus blue.

Explain how, when collecting a gas jar of ammonia, you could show when the gas jar was full.

3 Table 18.1 compares the properties of two gases **A** and **B** produced when lead(II) nitrate crystals are heated.

Colour	Colourless
Smell	Strong smell of rotten eggs
Solubility in cold water	Quite soluble
Solubility in hot water	Almost insoluble
Density at 25°C	1.4 g per dm^3
Melting point	$-83°C$
Boiling point	$-61°C$

Table 18.2 Properties of hydrogen sulphide

(a) Is it possible to collect the gas over cold water? Explain your answer. How could the method be altered to make it more suitable for collection of hydrogen sulphide?

(b) How could a dry sample of hydrogen sulphide be collected?

Gas	Density i.e. mass per dm^3	Solubility in water	Melting point °C	Boiling point °C
A	1.33 g	Almost insoluble	-218	-183
B	1.9 g	Very soluble		22

(Density of air is approximately 1.2 g per dm^3)

Table 18.1 Comparing the properties of two gases produced when lead(II) nitrate is heated

Draw a labelled diagram to show how both **A** and **B** can be collected when some crystals of lead(II) nitrate are heated in a test tube.

4 Jeanette heated a solid in a test tube and collected the gas produced over water. After several minutes, although the substance had changed in appearance, no gas had been collected. Explain why no gas had been collected.

5 Hydrogen sulphide is a gas and some of its properties are summarized in Table 18.2.

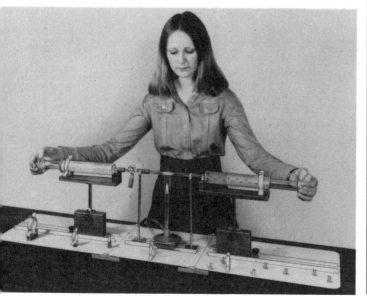

Fig. 18.5 A pupil using a gas syringe

Summary

The method used to collect a gas depends upon the properties of the gas.

If the gas does not dissolve in water it can be collected over water providing it is not required dry.

If the gas is denser than air it is collected by downward delivery and if less dense than air by upward delivery.

Unit 19

Heating Common Substances

In this unit we are going to consider the changes which take place when substances are heated in a Bunsen burner flame. The changes which take place when eight substances are heated are summarized in Figs. 19.1 and 19.2.

For each substance there are five boxes. In box 1 the original appearance of the substance is described. In box 2 the change on heating is described and in box 3 the changes which occur on cooling to room temperature are given. In box 4 the name of the substance formed is given and in box 5 is given the mass change which occurs.

19.1 Action of heat on common substances

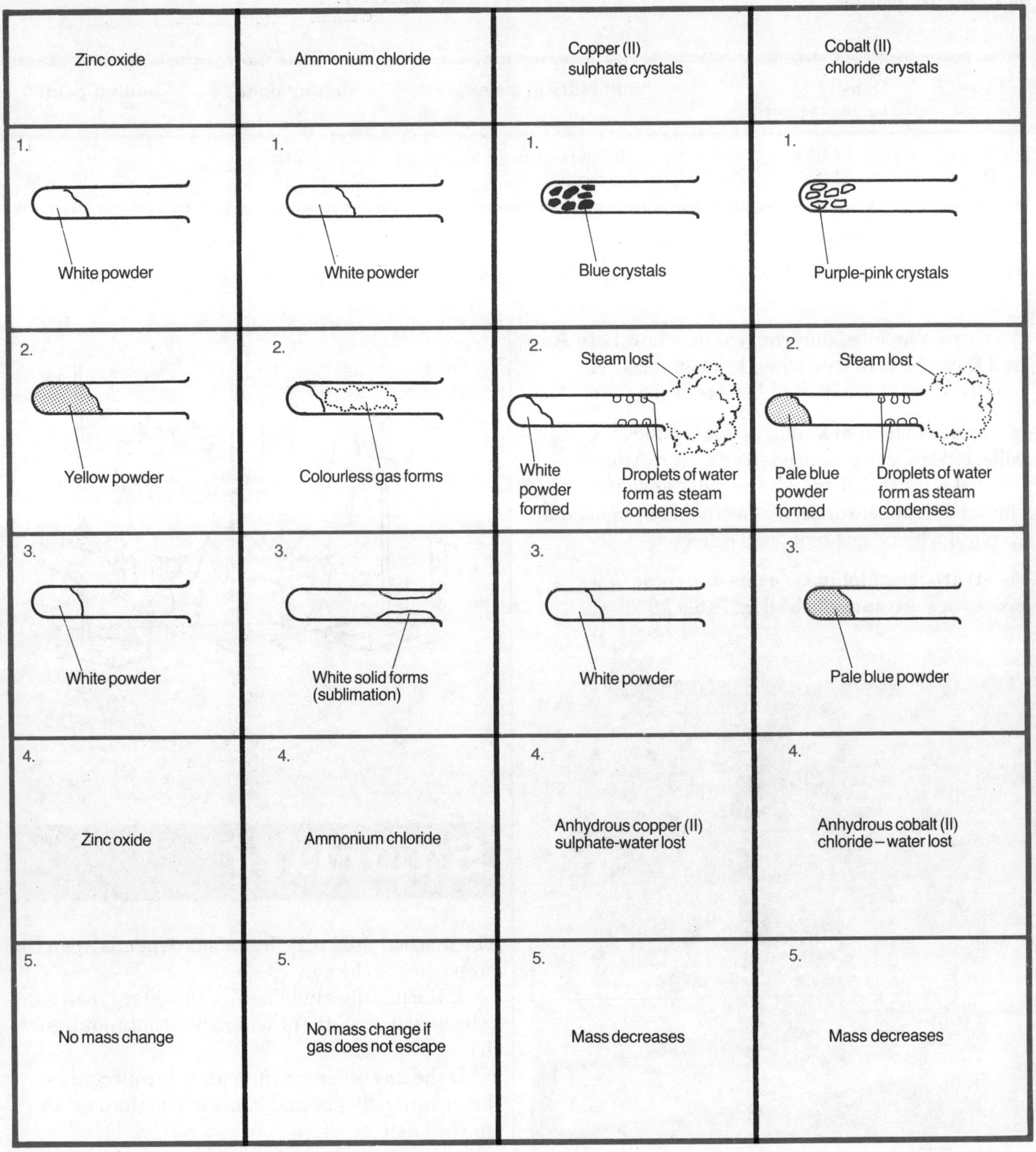

Zinc oxide	Ammonium chloride	Copper (II) sulphate crystals	Cobalt (II) chloride crystals
1. White powder	1. White powder	1. Blue crystals	1. Purple-pink crystals
2. Yellow powder	2. Colourless gas forms	2. Steam lost White powder formed — Droplets of water form as steam condenses	2. Steam lost Pale blue powder formed — Droplets of water form as steam condenses
3. White powder	3. White solid forms (sublimation)	3. White powder	3. Pale blue powder
4. Zinc oxide	4. Ammonium chloride	4. Anhydrous copper (II) sulphate – water lost	4. Anhydrous cobalt (II) chloride – water lost
5. No mass change	5. No mass change if gas does not escape	5. Mass decreases	5. Mass decreases

Fig. 19.1 The changes that take place when different substances are heated and then cooled

19.2 Mass changes which occur on heating

The mass changes which may be obtained during these heating experiments are very small. An accurate balance is necessary to notice these changes. The test tube or crucible is weighed accurately before heating and again when the temperature has returned to room temperature.

Mass changes which occur are discussed in greater detail in Unit 21.

19.3 Accurate observation

In any practical assessment or examination you might take in school you must observe all changes carefully and record them accurately. If you see a yellow powder, for example, you should try to find a suitable 'describing word' (adjective) to make your description more exact. For example, lemon yellow, pale yellow, etc.

Activities overleaf

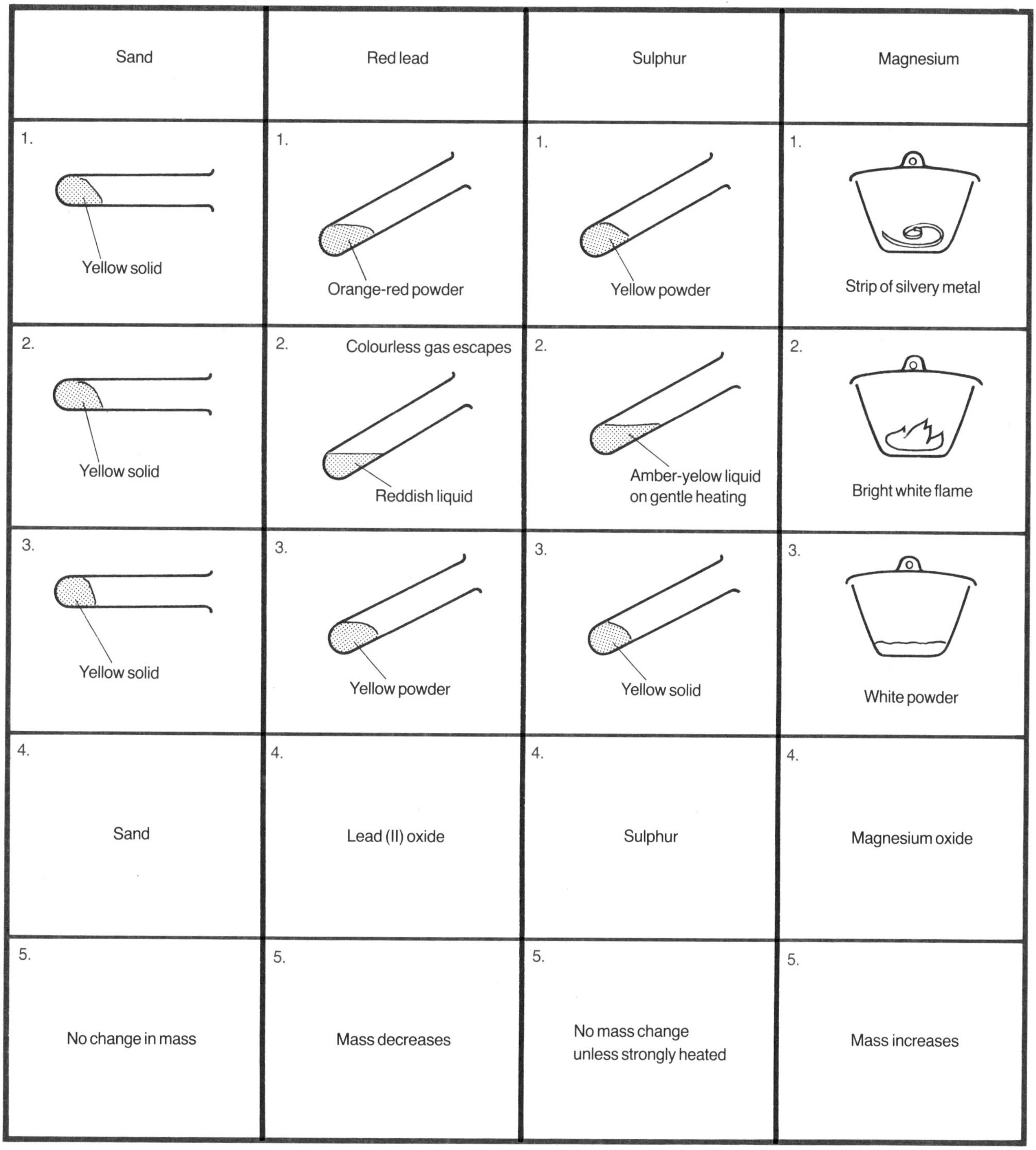

Sand	Red lead	Sulphur	Magnesium
1. Yellow solid	1. Orange-red powder	1. Yellow powder	1. Strip of silvery metal
2. Yellow solid	2. Colourless gas escapes Reddish liquid	2. Amber-yelow liquid on gentle heating	2. Bright white flame
3. Yellow solid	3. Yellow powder	3. Yellow solid	3. White powder
4. Sand	4. Lead (II) oxide	4. Sulphur	4. Magnesium oxide
5. No change in mass	5. Mass decreases	5. No mass change unless strongly heated	5. Mass increases

Fig. 19.2 The changes that take place when different substances are heated and then cooled

Activities

1 Below are descriptions of the action of heat on four different substances. Draw a chart like Fig. 19.1 including the information below.

Potassium permanganate is a dark purple crystalline solid. On heating a fine black powder is lost and also a colourless gas. A very dark green solid remains called potassium manganate.

Copper is a gold-coloured metal. On heating it glows red and, on cooling, a black coating is found on the surface of the copper. The black coating is copper(II) oxide.

Sodium carbonate crystals are transparent, colourless crystals. On heating a white powder is formed and droplets of colourless liquid condense on the cool part of the tube. Steam is also seen escaping from the test tube. On cooling, a white powder called anhydrous sodium carbonate remains.

Iodine crystals are dark, greyish black shiny crystals. On heating they quickly melt and immediately give off a purple gas. This gas cools further up the test tube to reform iodine crystals.

Name one substance in Fig. 19.1 or 19.2 which closely resembles each of these substances.

2 Which substance in Fig. 19.1 or 19.2
 (i) is unchanged on heating?
 (ii) sublimes on heating?
 (iii) is heated in a crucible rather than a test tube?

3 When heating magnesium the crucible lid has to be lifted from time to time.
 (i) Why is there a lid on the crucible?
 (ii) Why is it necessary to lift the lid of the crucible from time to time?

4 The changes which occur to the substances in Figs. 19.1 and 19.2 can be classified as **temporary** or **permanent** changes.

A **temporary change** is a change which can easily be reversed either by cooling or mixing all the products together. If ice is heated it turns to liquid water. If the water is cooled, ice is reformed.

A **permanent change** is one which cannot be reversed either by cooling or mixing the products. Once it has taken place it cannot be reversed. Burning a piece of wood is a permanent change. (N.B. In some books the terms physical and chemical change are used rather than temporary and permanent change.)

Complete Table 19.1 by putting each of the substances in Figs. 19.1 and 19.2 which change on heating into the correct column.

5 Red lead gives off a colourless gas when heated. This gas does not dissolve in water. Draw a diagram of apparatus which could be used to make some of this gas from red lead and collect a couple of test tubes of the gas.

6 Anhydrous copper(II) sulphate is a white powder which is produced when blue copper(II) sulphate crystals are heated and the water is driven off.

If some anhydrous copper(II) sulphate is put on a watch glass and drops of water are added, an interesting change takes place (Fig. 19.1). The watch glass gets very hot as heat is produced from the reaction between anhydrous copper(II) sulphate and water. A reaction of this type is called an **exothermic** reaction. The colour change is from white back to blue and hydrated copper(II) sulphate is reformed.
(i) Why is it necessary to keep anhydrous copper(II) sulphate in a well stoppered bottle?
(ii) What is anhydrous copper(II) sulphate used for in the laboratory?

Permanent changes on heating	Temporary changes on heating
1 _____	1 _____
2 _____	2 _____
	3 _____
	4 _____
	5 _____

Table 19.1 Changes on heating

7 Strips of filter paper are dipped into a solution of cobalt(II) chloride and then thoroughly dried in an oven.

(i) What colour is the filter paper after dipping in the cobalt(II) chloride solution?

(ii) What colour is the filter paper after drying?

(iii) For what purpose is this paper produced?

8 Copper turns black when heated in a Bunsen burner flame.

Jamie thought that this black coating was soot from the flame and this explained why the copper gained in mass when heated. Which of the following investigations could either prove or disprove Jamie's theory?

(i) A piece of copper wire was heated by passing an electric current through it. The wire was heated in air and it turned black.

(ii) A piece of copper wire was heated by passing an electric current through it. This time, however, the wire was sealed inside a tube so that it could not come into contact with air. The wire got hot but a black coating was not formed and there was no change in mass.

(iii) A piece of copper wire was sealed inside a glass tube out of contact with the air. The tube was heated with a Bunsen burner flame but the flame could not come in contact with the copper. The copper did not turn black and did not increase in mass.

Why do you think copper turns black when heated in a Bunsen burner flame?

Why is the increase in mass when a piece of copper is heated even smaller than the increase in mass when a piece of magnesium burns?

9 An electric light bulb contains a very fine wire or filament made of tungsten. This is a metal with a very high melting point. When electricity passes through the filament the filament glows white hot. Inside the bulb there must be no air.

(a) Why is tungsten preferred to a cheaper metal such as iron?

(b) What happens if, due to a fault in manufacture, air is present inside the bulb?

*10 Making a small spirit lamp
You can buy a small spirit lamp burning methylated spirit from a good toyshop. This can be used, in place of a Bunsen burner, in Activities where heating is required. However, methylated spirit is very flammable and great care should be taken when using a spirit burner. A wet cloth should be kept ready which should be used to cover and extinguish any small fire that might occur.

You can make your own spirit lamp burning methylated spirit from a glass ink bottle, a cork which fits the neck of the bottle and a piece of 'wick' from an ironmonger's shop (or very thick string).

Get an adult to make a hole through the cork with a drill or skewer. Push the wick through the cork until about 5 mm of it is above the cork and the other end of the wick dips into about 1 cm depth of methylated spirit in the ink bottle (see Fig. 19.3). Carefully light the wick.

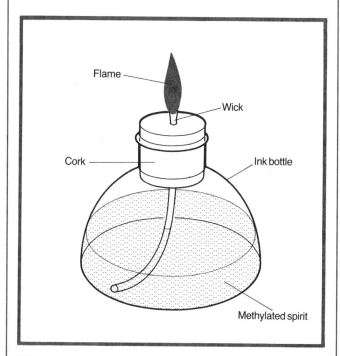

Fig. 19.3 A homemade spirit lamp

Summary

Many substances change in appearance on heating. Some of these changes are easily reversed and these changes are called temporary changes.

Other changes cannot be reversed and these are called permanent changes.

Unit 20

Air and its composition

Air is something that we take for granted. It is essential for life and we often forget that it is there. Air is, in fact, a mixture of gases. As a mixture its composition can vary from place to place.

20.1 Composition of air

A typical sample of air contains the following gases by volume:

Nitrogen	78%
Oxygen	21%
Carbon dioxide	0.03%
Argon	0.9%
Helium	0.0005%
Neon	0.002%
Krypton	0.0001%
Xenon	0.00001%

The amount of water vapour is variable.

The composition of air may be represented by a 'pie chart' (Fig. 20.1).

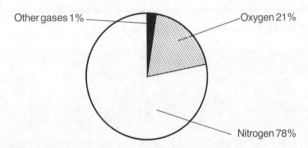

Fig. 20.1 Composition of air by volume

The most frequent mistake made by pupils is to state that there is a significant amount of hydrogen in air. This is not so.

Of the gases in the air, oxygen is the active gas. Most changes which take place involving air use up oxygen. The other gases are inactive.

20.2 Separating air into its constituent gases

Separating air into its constituent gases is not easy to do and cannot be done in the laboratory.

It is, however, important in the chemical industry to do this as all of the gases in air are valuable as pure gases. The separation is carried out by fractional distillation (Unit 10) of liquid air.

First, carbon dioxide and water vapour are removed from the air by cooling in a refrigeration plant. Both are easily frozen out and removed. If they were not removed first they would freeze in the pipes and block them.

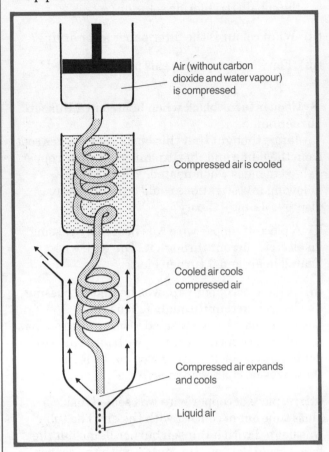

Fig. 20.2 Producing liquid air

The air is then liquefied (Fig. 20.2). You will know that compressing a gas makes it heat up. When you pump up a bicycle tyre, the tyre heats up. The air is compressed to about 150 times atmospheric pressure. The compressed air is then cooled.

The compressed air is then allowed to expand through a small hole. As it expands the air cools rapidly. The cooled air is used to cool more compressed air. The process is repeated until the temperature is about −200°C. At this temperature most of the air is liquid.

Finally, the liquid air is allowed to warm up.

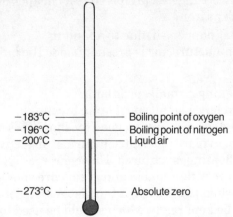

Fig. 20.3 Air liquefies at a very low temperature

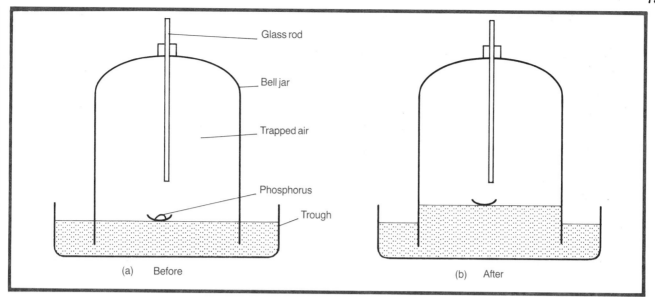

Fig. 20.4 (a) Apparatus used to find the approximate percentage of oxygen in air

Fig 20.4 (b) After the phosphorus has burned the water level rises

Nitrogen boils off first because it has a lower boiling point than oxygen (Fig. 20.3).

A fractional distillation plant can separate about 100 tonnes of air a day.

20.3 The percentage of oxygen in air

(i) An approximate method

Phosphorus burns in air to form phosphorus oxide. When it burns it uses up only the oxygen in the air. The phosphorus oxide which forms dissolves in water.

The apparatus is set up as in Fig. 20.4(a) with air trapped inside the bell jar. A small piece of phosphorus floats in a crucible on the water. The phosphorus is set alight by touching it with a hot glass rod. The phosphorus burns and the phosphorus oxide formed dissolves in the water. The water level rises one fifth of the way up the bell jar, showing that approximately one fifth of the air has been used up (Fig. 20.4b).

(ii) An accurate method

Two gas syringes are connected to opposite ends of a piece of hard glass tubing. The hard glass tubing is filled with pieces of copper and 100 cm³ of air is trapped in one of the syringes. The other syringe contains no air (Fig. 20.5a).

The hard glass tube is heated and the air is passed backwards and forwards from one syringe to the other. (See also Fig. 18.5.)

The copper reacts with the oxygen in the sample of air and forms a black coating of copper oxide (Unit 19).

When no further change is taking place, the apparatus is allowed to cool to room temperature. About 80 cm³ of air remain (Fig. 20.5b). This shows that in the 100 cm³ sample of air there are 20 cm³ of oxygen – the active gas.

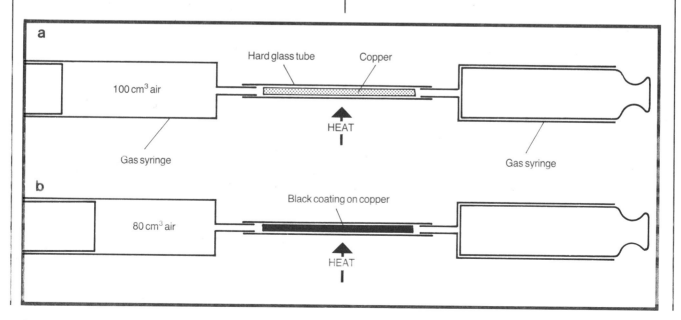

Fig. 20.5 (a) Apparatus used to find the percentage of oxygen in air accurately
Fig. 20.5 (b) Heating causes the copper to react with the oxygen in the air sample

74

Activities

1 Table 20.1 lists the boiling points of the gases remaining in air after carbon dioxide and water vapour are removed.

Gas	Boiling point °C
Xenon	−108
Krypton	−153
Oxygen	−183
Argon	−186
Nitrogen	−196
Neon	−246
Helium	−269

Table 20.1 Boiling points of some of the gases in air

(a) Which gas in Table 20.1 would be produced in the largest volume by the fractional distillation of liquid air?

(b) Which gas in Table 20.1 has the highest boiling point?

(c) Which gases in Table 20.1 would not be liquid at −200°C?

(d) Neon, argon, krypton, xenon and helium (the noble gases) are sometimes called the 'rare gases'. Looking at Fig. 20.1, is this a fair statement?

2 Figs. 20.6 and 20.7 show oxygen and nitrogen gases being used. For each photograph

(i) state whether it is oxygen or nitrogen being used;

(ii) give the use illustrated by the photograph.

*3 In this activity you can find the percentage of oxygen in air. Oxygen is used up when iron rusts.

Take a test tube and rinse it out with cold water. Push a small piece of steel wool into the test tube. Turn the test tube upside down and stand it in water in a dish (see Fig. 20.8a). Leave the apparatus set up for a week. At the end of the week the water level in the test tube should have risen (Fig. 20.8b). By measuring the distances **x** and **y** before and after the investigation you should be able to work out the percentage of oxygen in the air.

4 An investigation was carried out using the apparatus in Fig. 20.5. Before and after the investigation the hard glass tube and contents were weighed. The results were:

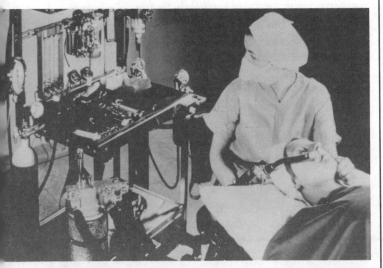

Fig. 20.6 (a)

Fig. 20.6 (b)

Fig. 20.7 (a)

Fig. 20.7 (b)

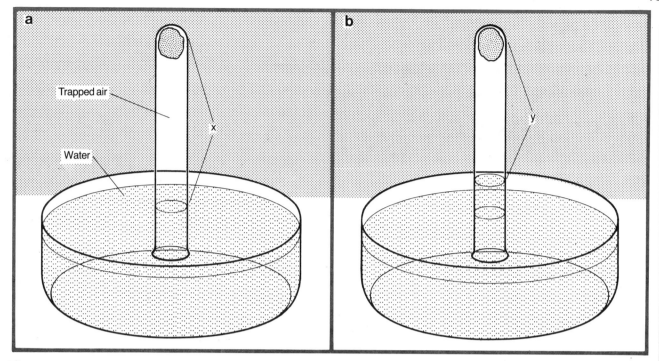

Fig. 20.8 (a) Finding the percentage
of oxygen in air

Fig. 20.8 (b) The water level after a week

Mass of hard glass tube and copper before
heating = 59.245 g
Mass of hard glass tube and contents after
heating = 59.272 g
Volume of air in the syringe before = 100 cm^3
Volume of gas in the syringe after = 80 cm^3

(a) What volume of gas was removed from the air
during the experiment?

(b) What was the gain in mass of the hard glass
tube and contents during the experiment?

(c) The gain in mass of the hard glass tube and
contents is the same as the loss of mass of the gas
in the syringe.
What is the mass of the gas lost from the syringe?
Work out the mass of 1000 cm^3 of the gas lost
from the syringe.

(d) Table 20.2 gives the mass of 1000 cm^3 of
different gases at room temperature and pressure.
What do the results of the experiment confirm?

Gas	Mass of 1000 cm^3 of different gases g
Hydrogen	0.09
Helium	0.17
Nitrogen	1.17
Oxygen	1.33
Carbon dioxide	1.83
Sulphur dioxide	2.67

Table 20.2 The masses of 1000 cm^3 of six gases under the
same conditions of temperature and pressure

Summary

Air is a mixture of gases. The active gas in air is
oxygen (about one fifth of air by volume). By far
the commonest gas in air is nitrogen which is
inactive. Other gases include carbon dioxide,
argon, neon, krypton and xenon. There is no
hydrogen in air. The composition of air varies
from place to place.

Air can be separated into its constituent gases
by fractional distillation of liquid air. This relies
on the different boiling points of these gases.

The percentage of oxygen in air is best found
by a syringe experiment. A fixed volume of air is
passed over heated copper and the oxygen is
removed.

Unit 21

Processes involving air

There are a number of everyday processes which involve air. These include burning (or combustion), breathing (or respiration), rusting and photosynthesis. In this unit we are going to consider these processes in some detail.

21.1 Burning (or combustion)

The burning (or combustion) of a substance is the combining of a substance with oxygen. Burning usually produces heat and/or light.

Burning, therefore, requires air or oxygen and, if the supply is cut off, burning will stop (see Fire extinguishers in Volume 2, Unit 17.).

Although it does not always seem to be so, the combined mass of all the substances produced is always greater than the mass of the substance burned.

21.2 Burning metals and non-metals

A wide range of substances burn in air or oxygen. In Table 21.1 the burning of some metals and non-metals is compared. The burning of these substances in oxygen can be carried out using the apparatus in Fig. 21.1.

From these and similar investigations the following conclusions can be made.

(i) Substances burn better in oxygen than in air.

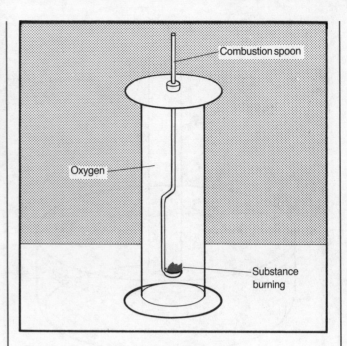

Fig. 21.1 Burning a substance in oxygen

Fig. 21.2 A candle burning in trapped air

	Combustion in air	Combustion in oxygen	pH of residue	Name of residue
Magnesium	Burns brightly with a white flame	Burns brightly with a white flame	11 (strongly alkaline)	Magnesium oxide (a small amount of magnesium nitride is also formed when magnesium burns in air)
Sulphur	Burns with a very small blue flame	Burns with a bigger blue flame	4 (acidic)	Sulphur dioxide
Copper	No noticeable flame Copper glows red hot		7 (neutral)	Coating of copper(II) oxide
Carbon	Glows red	Glows brighter	5.5 (slightly acidic)	Carbon dioxide
Iron wool	Glows red	Burns well	7 (neutral)	Iron oxide

Table 21.1 The results of burning some metals and non-metals

(ii) Metal burns in oxygen to form oxides which are neutral or alkaline (pH 7 or greater).

(iii) Non-metals burn in oxygen to form oxides which are acidic (pH less than 7).

21.3 Combustion of a candle

Candle wax is made up from carbon and hydrogen in the form of a hydrocarbon. When a hydrocarbon burns the substances produced include carbon dioxide and water.

If a dry beaker is turned upside down and stood over a burning candle (Fig. 21.2) the candle continues to burn. After a while the flame starts to falter and then goes out. Inside the beaker soot (carbon) may be seen. Also water condenses into droplets on the inside of the beaker.

The candle goes out when the concentration of oxygen inside the beaker drops below a certain level.

21.4 Respiration

Respiration is very closely related to combustion. In the body food 'burns' in oxygen to form carbon dioxide and water. The oxygen is obtained from the air we breathe in. It is transported around the body by the blood to the muscles. Here 'burning' takes place and carbon dioxide is produced.

The air we breathe out contains much less oxygen and much more carbon dioxide than the air we breathe in.

The heat produced in our bodies by the 'burning' of our food helps to keep our body temperature constant.

21.5 Rusting

Many metals corrode when left exposed to the air. Of the common pure metals only silver and gold do not corrode. The corrosion of iron and steel is particularly important and is called rusting.

The rusting of iron is a slower process than burning but it also uses up oxygen. In Fig. 21.3

a series of investigations is shown to find out what substances must be present for rusting to take place.

The four test tubes are set up as follows:

(i) An iron nail is put into water. The nail is in contact with air and water. This tube is being used as a **control**.

(ii) Anhydrous calcium chloride removes all the water vapour from the air. The nail is in contact with air but not water.

(iii) The distilled water is boiled before use to remove any dissolved air. The nail is in contact with water but not with air.

(iv) The nail is in an oil. It is out of contact with air and water.

The results are summarized in Table 21.2.

Test tube number	Observations
1	Rust
2	No rust
3	No rust
4	No rust

Table 21.2 Results obtained in an experiment on rusting

From these observations we can conclude that *both* air and water must be present if rusting is to take place. It is, in fact, oxygen in the air which, along with water, causes rusting. Other substances such as carbon dioxide or salt may speed up the rusting process.

Rust is a very complicated chemical. It is, in fact, a hydrated iron oxide.

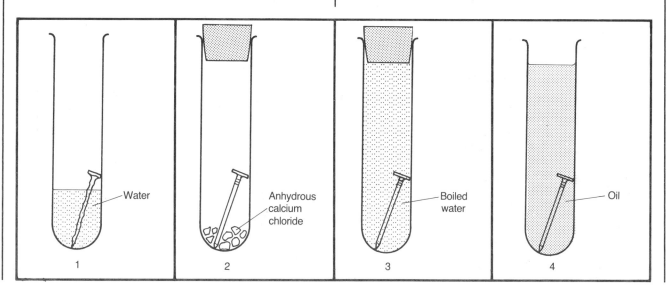

Fig. 21.3 Rusting of iron

Unit 21 continued

21.6 Methods of preventing rust

Rusting is an extremely important process. It costs many million pounds each year.

One of the commonest ways of preventing rust is painting. A film of paint covers the iron and prevents air and water vapour coming into contact with the iron. Unfortunately, if the paint film is broken, rusting will take place under the paint film. Modern paints have much improved the situation but regular painting is still necessary.

Iron or steel can be coated with plastic to prevent rusting. A washing-up rack, for example, uses this type of protection.

Parts of an engine or woodworking tools cannot be painted and may be protected by coating the metal with a thin layer of oil or grease.

Iron can be coated with a layer of the metal zinc in a process called **galvanizing**. The zinc can be scratched but the iron does not rust. Zinc-based paints can also be used as 'primer' paints to undercoat when painting iron railings, etc.

Food cans are made of steel coated with a thin layer of tin. If the tin coating is scratched the steel continues to rust under the coating.

Fig. 21.4 shows how the steel legs of a pier can be protected from damage by rust. The blocks of the metal magnesium corrode away and are replaced. While they corrode they protect the steel and it does not rust.

21.7 Photosynthesis

Combustion, respiration and rusting all use up oxygen. Why do we never run out of oxygen?

Fortunately, the process of photosynthesis produces oxygen to replace the oxygen which is used up.

Green plants take in carbon dioxide and give out oxygen. The carbon dioxide and water taken in through the roots react together to produce carbohydrates and oxygen. This process, called photosynthesis, only takes place in strong sunlight. A chemical called chlorophyll in the plant also assists the process.

If the amount of vegetation on the earth was reduced it would reduce the amount of photosynthesis which could take place and could alter the amount of oxygen in the air.

Strips of magnesium are lowered into the water alongside each leg

Fig. 21.4 Protecting the legs of a pier

Activities

1 A series of investigations was carried out to find the mass changes when different masses of magnesium were burnt in air. Six groups each carried out an experiment but with a different mass of magnesium ribbon.

The magnesium was put into a crucible. The mass of the crucible, lid and magnesium was found. The crucible was heated strongly.

From time to time the lid of the crucible was lifted. After burning had finished the crucible, lid and contents were allowed to cool to room temperature before reweighing. The results of the six groups are shown in Table 21.3.

Group	Mass of magnesium	Mass of residue
I	0.09 g	0.15 g
II	0.12 g	0.20 g
III	0.15 g	0.25 g
IV	0.18 g	0.30 g
V	0.21 g	0.32 g
VI	0.24 g	0.40 g

Table 21.3 Mass changes when different masses of magnesium were burnt in air

(a) Name the residue formed when magnesium burns in air.

(b) Why was the lid of the crucible lifted from time to time?

(c) Plot the results of each group on the graph shown in Fig. 21.5. Put a small cross on the graph for each group. The result for group I has been plotted for you.

(d) Draw the best straight line you can. Your line will go through most of the crosses.

(e) Which group's results were inaccurate?

(f) What mass of residue would be formed if 0.11 g of magnesium was burned?

2 An investigation was carried out to compare the time it took for a candle flame to go out when it was covered with beakers of different sizes. The results are shown plotted on the graph in Fig. 21.6.

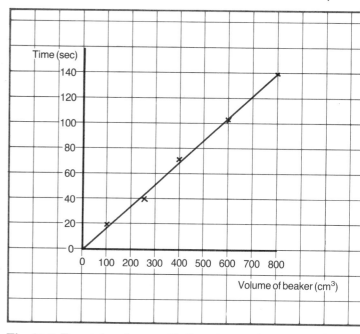

Fig. 21.6 Time taken for a candle flame to go out when covered with beakers of different sizes

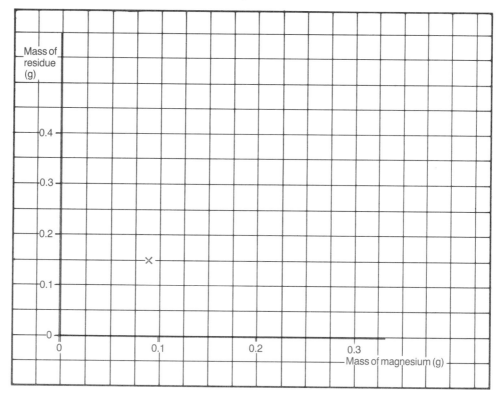

Fig. 21.5 Mass changes when different masses of magnesium were burnt in air

Activities continued

(a) How long would it take for a candle to go out if covered with a 500 cm^3 beaker?

(b) The results plotted do not all fall exactly on the graph drawn. Why do you think this is so?

(c) What can be concluded from these results? As the volume of air trapped under the beaker increases the time taken for the candle flame to go out _____.

(d) Explain the conclusion that you made in (c).

Mrs Evans, the teacher, is trying to convince the class that when a candle burns there is an increase in mass. It does not seem very likely!

She explains that this is only so if all of the substances formed are collected and weighed.

The apparatus in Fig. 21.7 was set up. The U-shaped tube contained a chemical called soda lime which absorbs both carbon dioxide and water

*4 Tests with a solution of limewater.
Make a solution of limewater by adding some hydrated lime (calcium hydroxide – from a garden shop) to water in a test tube. Shake the test tube thoroughly. Leave the solution to stand until the undissolved solid settles to the bottom.

Carefully pour some of the clear solution into another test tube. This is a solution of limewater.

Put the end of a drinking straw into the limewater and *gently* blow through the solution. Observe carefully all the changes which take place.

Which gas in the air you breathe out is causing these changes?

*5 Put a clean steel nail into a test tube and add tap water until the nail is partly covered with

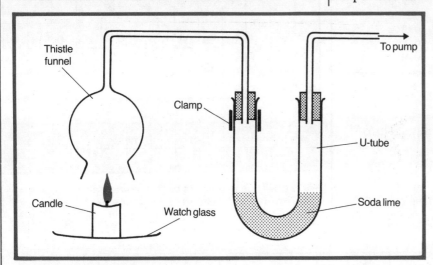

Fig. 21.7 Mrs Evans's apparatus

Fig. 21.8 Can you explain what happens to the nail?

vapour. The whole apparatus including the candle and watch glass was weighed accurately.

Air was drawn through the apparatus with a pump for a few minutes, with the candle alight. When the apparatus had cooled to room temperature the entire apparatus, watch glass and candle were reweighed. The results were:

Mass of apparatus before = 132.35 g
Mass of apparatus after   = 132.65 g

(a) What was the increase in mass?

(b) Where did this increase in mass come from?

(c) Claire pointed out to the class that the increase in mass might be caused only by gases in the air and have nothing to do with the candle burning.

Which two gases did Claire mean?

(d) How could Mrs Evans show the class that this was not true and the increase in mass was due to the candle burning?

water (Fig. 21.8). Leave the test tube for some days. Observe carefully the changes which take place. How do you explain your observations?

Repeat this experiment with salt water in place of tap water.

You can carry out similar investigations with steel nails and tap water but put either a small piece of copper (from electric wires) or a piece of zinc (from the case of a torch battery) into the test tube in contact with the nail.

Why would it be unwise to use a copper washer between two pieces of steel exhaust pipe?

6 Modern car makers go to great lengths to rustproof their cars. By looking in a car magazine or catalogue, write down various methods they use to prevent rusting.

*__7__ Set up the apparatus in Fig. 21.9 with some water-weed under the funnel. Stand the apparatus in a sunny place for a few days. Bubbles of a colourless gas collect in the test tube.

If you can collect a test tube full of gas, test the gas by putting a glowing splint into it. What do you observe?

When setting up a garden pond you have to put green plants called 'oxygenators' into the pond.

What is the purpose of these plants?

8 There are extensive rain forests in Brazil. The trees and plants in these forests are extremely important as they provide a large amount of oxygen.

(a) Name the process which produces oxygen.

(b) Imagine all the rain forests were destroyed by a fire. What could be the results of this fire?

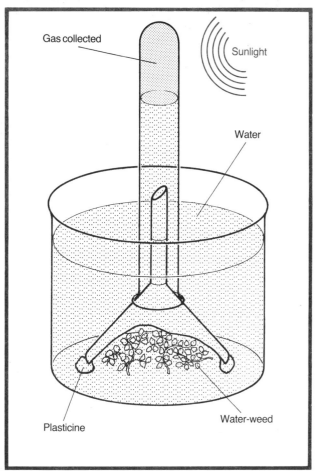

Fig. 21.9 What gas has been collected?

Summary

Components of air	Combustion	Rusting	Breathing	Photosynthesis
Nitrogen	Usually not involved	Not involved	Not involved	Not involved
Oxygen	Usually necessary	Necessary	Necessary	Produced
Carbon dioxide	Formed if substances containing carbon burn	Speeds up rusting but it is not necessary	Produced	Necessary
Noble gases	No effect			
Water vapour	Formed if substances containing hydrogen burn	Necessary	Produced	Necessary

Unit 22

Oxygen (1)

Oxygen is frequently needed for investigations in the laboratory. Often we get it from a cylinder of gas.

In this unit we are going to consider how we can make some test tubes of oxygen from chemicals in the laboratory. This is sometimes called the laboratory preparation of oxygen.

22.1 Laboratory preparation of oxygen

Oxygen can be made from a liquid called hydrogen peroxide. This is a mild bleach which splits up on standing to produce water and oxygen.

The oxygen is produced more quickly if certain substances called **catalysts** are added. One catalyst is manganese(IV) oxide (sometimes called manganese dioxide). This is a black powder. A catalyst quickens the splitting up but is not used

up itself. A small amount of catalyst can produce a large volume of oxygen.

We can summarize the change as follows:

Hydrogen Peroxide $\xrightarrow{\text{manganese(IV) oxide}}$ Water + Oxygen

Fig. 22.1 shows the apparatus which could be used to produce and collect a few test tubes of oxygen gas.

It is easy to show that the gas produced is oxygen. If a burning splint is blown out it will continue to glow. This is called a glowing splint. When a glowing splint is put into oxygen the splint relights. This is the test for oxygen.

22.2 Other substances producing oxygen

Oxygen is commonly produced when substances are heated. Substances which produce oxygen on heating include:

**potassium permanganate
red lead
potassium nitrate
mercury oxide**

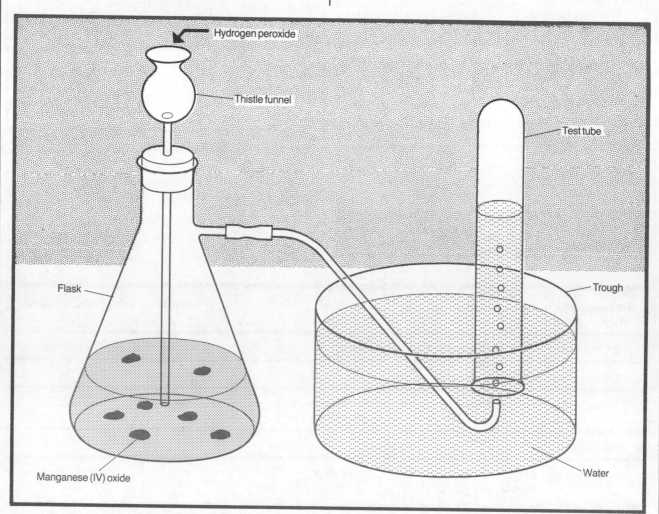

Fig. 22.1 Laboratory preparation of oxygen

Activities

1 Fig. 22.1 shows a three-dimensional diagram to show how oxygen can be produced from hydrogen peroxide.

(a) Draw a labelled section diagram to show how oxygen can be prepared.

(b) The first couple of test tubes of gas collected did not relight a glowing splint. Why is this?

(c) How could the manganese(IV) oxide be recovered from the contents of the flask at the end of the experiment?

2 Hydrogen peroxide can be a dangerous chemical. A bottle of hydrogen peroxide was left standing on a sunny window sill. The bottle had a screw top. Suddenly one day the bottle exploded and the fragments of glass went right across the room.

Why did the bottle explode?

How would you recommend hydrogen peroxide to be stored?

3 Oxygen is produced when red lead is heated. Using the apparatus in Fig. 22.2, draw a section diagram to show how a sample of oxygen could be prepared and collected when red lead is heated.

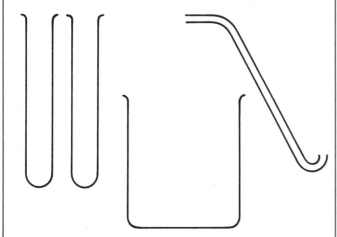

Fig. 22.2 Draw a diagram to show how this apparatus is used to obtain a sample of oxygen when red lead is heated

*4 You can buy hydrogen peroxide at a good chemist but do be careful with it. Do not spill the liquid. Put a little hydrogen peroxide into a test tube and add a small piece of raw liver to the test tube. What do you observe? (This investigation requires the supervision of an adult.)

5 The answers to most of the clues in the following crossword will be found in Units 20–22.

Fig. 22.3 Now try this puzzle

Across
1. A bitterly pungent smell.
2. A metal which rusts.
7. Oxides of non-metals are usually _____.
9. A process using up oxygen.
10. Chemical abbreviation for a shiny metal on handlebars.
11. Formed when a substance burns.
12. Chemical abbreviation for a gas in the air.
13. An inactive gas in the air.
17. A metal used to plate food cans.
18. pH 7

Down
2. Non-metal oxides may turn litmus this colour.
3. Carbon _____ is required before photosynthesis can take place.
4. Chemical abbreviation for a metal used for galvanizing.
6. The active gas in the air.
8. Rusting is an example of this.
14. A lighted splint will go _____ if put into nitrogen gas.
15. Estimated time of arrival (abbreviation).
16. The volume of hydrogen in a volume of air.

Summary

Oxygen can be prepared in the laboratory by the splitting up of hydrogen peroxide.

Hydrogen peroxide $\xrightarrow{\text{manganese(IV) oxide}}$ **water + oxygen**

Manganese(IV) oxide speeds up the change and is called a catalyst.

Unit 23

Oxygen (2)

History of its discovery

*T*his unit considers work done by famous chemists in the 18th century. This was an exciting time in Chemistry when rapid progress was being made. We can learn a great deal about Chemistry by studying the work of famous chemists.

23.1 The discovery of oxygen

Although oxygen is all around us it was not recognized until the 18th century. Oxygen was first discovered by Wilhelm Scheele in 1773. He was Swedish. He called the gas 'fire air' because substances burned well in it. His book explaining his discovery was called *Air and Fire*. It did not, however, appear until 1777.

In the meantime, in England, Joseph Priestley discovered oxygen without knowing anything about the work of Scheele. He reported his discovery to a public meeting of the British Royal Society on 23 March 1775. Because Scheele's experiments had not been published at this time, we usually give the credit for the discovery of oxygen to Priestley. This perhaps shows the importance of accurate note taking and speedy action in our experimental work!

Fig 23.1 Priestley's apparatus for investigation of gases, 1775

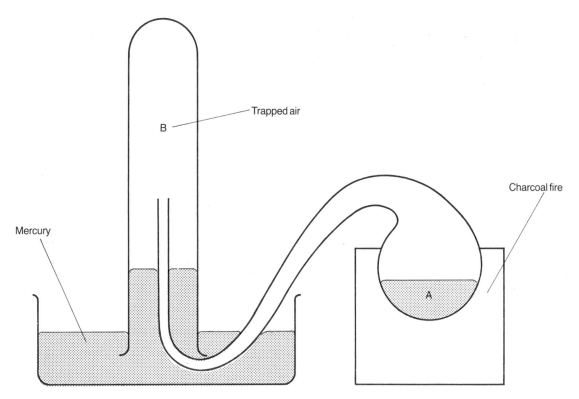

Fig. 23.2 Lavoisier's apparatus

Priestley had been given a large magnifying glass as a present. On 1 August 1774 he used the sun and his magnifying glass to heat a number of substances. One substance he heated was mercury. This is a silvery coloured liquid. Red powdery particles formed on the mercury. He carefully removed these red particles and heated them alone. A colourless gas was produced. He found that:

(i)   a candle burned better in the gas than in air;

(ii) a mouse in the gas was very lively;

(iii) a piece of smouldering charcoal burst into flames.

He called this gas, which we now call oxygen, 'dephlogisticated air' – a rather lengthy name!

Priestley visited the famous French chemist Lavoisier in Paris and told him of his discovery. It was Lavoisier who gave the gas the name 'oxygen' in 1787. Priestley's discovery led to further progress by Lavoisier in finding out about what happens when a substance burns.

23.2 The theory of combustion

At this time it was believed that when a substance burns it loses a substance called 'phlogiston'. The residue remaining was called a 'calx'. This was called the phlogiston theory. A substance which would not burn, e.g. sand, contained no phlogiston. This theory, however, did not explain why a substance such as mercury increases in mass when it loses phlogiston!

Lavoisier was very interested in Priestley's experiments and repeated them carefully.

He heated some mercury in the apparatus in Fig. 23.2 for a number of days. He noticed that

approximately one fifth of the air trapped in **B** had disappeared and the red powder was on the top of the mercury.

He carefully removed the red powder and weighed it. He then heated it alone and collected the gas which was produced. He weighed the amount of mercury which had been produced.

He found that the red powder had decreased in mass. Also the volume of oxygen collected was the same as the volume of air which was lost in the first experiment.

He concluded that the mercury increased in mass because it had combined with the oxygen in the air. Today we would summarize this as:

Mercury + Oxygen → Mercury Oxide

Activities

Joseph Priestley (1733–1804)

Joseph Priestley was born in Fieldhead, near Leeds, on 13 March 1733. His parents were very religious and it was no surprise when, in 1755, he became a minister of the church. In 1760 he became a teacher of classics and literature in a private school in Warrington.

On a visit to London he met Benjamin Franklin. On his return he wrote a *History of Electricity* and was admitted to the Royal Society in 1766.

Living next to a brewery, he became interested in the heavy air which lay over the fermentation vats. He also studied the gas given off when acid is added to chalk. In both cases the gas is carbon dioxide and his studies led to him being awarded the Copley medal by the Royal Society in 1773.

In 1772 he discovered nitrogen and called it 'phlogisticated air'.

In 1780 Priestley became the minister of a church in Birmingham. While his scientific writings were highly regarded many of his religious writings made him unpopular with the public. In 1791 a mob destroyed his church and his house in Birmingham. He was forced to escape to Worcester in disguise.

He settled in London but was very unhappy. He emigrated to America where he had three sons living. He arrived in New York and was offered a professorship and a ministry. He refused both. He died in America in 1804.

Apart from the discovery of oxygen, Priestley greatly advanced methods of collecting and using gases.

Antoine Laurent Lavoisier (1743–1794)

Lavoisier was born in Paris on 26 August 1743 of wealthy parents. He was given an excellent education at the Collége Nazarin. He studied Mathematics, Astronomy, Chemistry and Botany.

In 1766 he received a gold medal from the Academy of Sciences. His award was for an essay on the best method of lighting a large town.

He graduated in Law and was appointed director of the Academy of Sciences in 1768. He carried out many scientific experiments. He considerably improved the manufacture of gunpowder.

In 1778 he set up an experimental farm to demonstrate the advantages of scientific agriculture.

He was elected to the assembly of Orleans in 1787. He made many efforts to improve the conditions of the ordinary people such as introducing saving schemes and purchasing supplies in times of famine.

He was secretary of the commission set up in 1790 to ensure that weights and measures were the same throughout France. This led to the introduction of the metric system.

Unfortunately, because of his wealth and importance, he became a target for the revolutionaries in the French Revolution. He was arrested in May 1794 and tried by a revolutionary court. The trial lasted only a few hours and he, and 27 others, were condemned to death. That afternoon they were guillotined and buried in a common grave.

Fig. 23.3 Joseph Priestley (1773–1804), the discoverer of oxygen (*above right*)

1 Read the account opposite and answer the questions.

(a) How old was Priestley when
  (i) he discovered oxygen?
  (ii) he was awarded the Copley medal?
  (iii) he died?

(b) Name three gases which Priestley experimented with.

(c) Priestley wrote of oxygen: 'It may be peculiarly salutary for the lungs in certain cases'.
  Give one use of oxygen which Priestley could foresee.

2 Imagine that you are Priestley. Write an imaginary letter to Lavoisier explaining excitedly your discovery of oxygen.

3 Read the passage opposite and answer the questions.

(a) How old was Lavoisier when
  (i) he received the gold medal?
  (ii) he set up the experimental farm?
  (iii) he was executed?

(b) Why did Lavoisier consider lighting a large town to be an important project at this time?

(c) You are very unlikely to see Lavoisier's experiments repeated exactly in your school laboratory. Why do you think this is so?

Summary

During the late 18th century great advances in the study of common gases were made. The names of Scheele, Priestley and Lavoisier in particular should be remembered.

Priestley discovered oxygen by heating mercury oxide. Lavoisier greatly advanced understanding of what happens when substances burn.

Two things worth remembering about these men are:

(i) The apparatus they used was very simple. They did not have the benefits of modern equipment.

(ii) They lived very full lives with many interests apart from Chemistry.

Fig. 23.4 Antoine Lavoisier (1743–94) (*left*)

Unit 24

Air pollution

Unit 20 considered the gases normally present in air. Other gases, however, can be found in the air and they can cause a variety of problems.

The presence of these substances in air is called **air pollution**.

In this unit we are going to consider different gases (or pollutants) which might be present in the air, where they might come from and the problems they cause.

24.1 Sulphur dioxide

Sulphur dioxide is the gas which is the major cause of air or atmospheric pollution. It is produced as a waste product during the burning of coal or fuel oil. Coal and fuel oil contain about 2% of sulphur and this forms sulphur dioxide on burning.

In the early 1950s sulphur dioxide, and the smoke which was always with it, produced great problems especially in large towns and cities. These substances caused blackening of buildings, long-term fogs and serious health problems. In one winter 4000 people died in London because of this pollution. In 1956 the Clean Air Act was passed by Parliament. This Act set up areas of cities called 'smokeless zones'. In 'smokeless zones' coal cannot be burned and smokeless fuels must be used. The result of this Act has been to improve greatly conditions in our cities.

Fig. 24.1 Effect of atmospheric pollution on stonework

© Crown copyright – reproduced with the permission of the Controller of Her Majesty's Stationery Office

Fig. 24.2 The large cooling towers of a power station produce mainly water vapour. Sulphur dioxide escapes through narrower chimneys

Sulphur dioxide dissolves in water to form sulphurous acid. In the presence of oxides of nitrogen, sulphurous acid can be converted into sulphuric acid. These acids, present in the air as fine droplets, can rapidly increase the corrosion of metals and the decay of stonework. They can also greatly affect the growth of plants.

When the Clean Air Act was passed the burning of coal in household fires was regarded as the major problem. House chimneys are comparatively low and sulphur dioxide and smoke emitted do not disperse. Factory chimneys today still emit smoke and sulphur dioxide but the chimneys are very high and it is hoped that any pollution disperses. When smoke is produced from a factory chimney fuel is being wasted – about 4% of fuel is lost in smoke. The sulphur dioxide still being lost through factory chimneys could be put to better use. If it could be removed efficiently it

London before and after the Clean Air Act (*left*)

could provide all the raw material necessary to produce sulphuric acid and save expensive imports of sulphur.

Today we are beginning to realize that this sulphur dioxide is still causing problems and there is great discussion about the effects of 'acid rain'.

24.2 Carbon monoxide

Carbon monoxide is a very poisonous gas produced by the partial burning of fuels. Most of the carbon monoxide in the air comes from car exhausts because the petrol is not efficiently burnt in the engine.

Close to heavy traffic the concentration of carbon monoxide in the air can reach 10–20 parts per million. Levels as high as 200 ppm have been recorded. Exposure of adults to levels in excess of 50 ppm can definitely be harmful. High concentrations prevent oxygen going round the body by destroying the red blood cells which do this job. Low concentrations are still harmful, possibly affecting the proper working of the brain.

24.3 Oxides of nitrogen

About 30–40% of the oxides of nitrogen in the air come from car exhausts. In the car engine nitrogen and oxygen, from the air, combine together to form these oxides of nitrogen.

Even very small amounts of these oxides of nitrogen can have serious effects on the environment. Like sulphur dioxide, they dissolve in water to form a mixture of acids – nitric and nitrous acids.

Apart from car exhausts, oxides of nitrogen are also emitted from certain factories and are produced naturally by lightning during thunderstorms.

24.4 Improving car exhausts

From the previous sections you will conclude that the car engine is a major cause for concern when thinking about pollution. The growth in the number of cars makes the problem worse.

It is possible to modify exhaust systems to reduce air pollution. In Fig. 24.3 a diagram of a modified engine and exhaust system is shown. The exhaust gases are passed through a converter. The converter contains a **catalyst**, such as platinum, which converts the harmful gases present into carbon dioxide, nitrogen, oxygen and water vapour. All these are normally present in air and therefore do not cause pollution.

24.5 Photochemical smog

Exhaust fumes from motor cars are causing additional problems in certain parts of the world. Strong sunlight acting upon the oxides of nitrogen, carbon monoxide and unused petrol vapour produce new and more unpleasant substances including a reactive form of oxygen called ozone. These acrid fumes collect in valleys and cause many problems. Apart from health problems this pollution also:

(i) causes the breakdown of plastics and rubber;
(ii) speeds up the fading of dyes.

At present there is no evidence of this photochemical smog in Great Britain but atmospheric pollution is being carefully watched. It is causing a problem in Los Angeles, Tokyo and Rotterdam.

24.6 Other substances in the air

Lead in a variety of forms can be present in the air. Most of this lead again comes from car exhausts. A substance called tetraethyl lead is added to petrol to improve its burning properties. This lead is lost in exhaust fumes. It is a very poisonous substance which affects the brain, especially of children.

There is considerable pressure for the removal of lead from petrol. This would slightly increase the price of petrol.

Asbestos in the form of tiny fibres may be present in the air. It can come from building materials and from car brake pads and discs. Recently the danger of exposure to asbestos has been realized. Certain types of asbestos fibre can cause certain types of cancer.

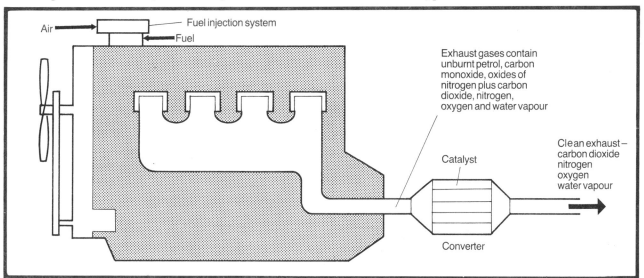

Fig. 24.3 An improved exhaust system for cars reduces air pollution

Activities

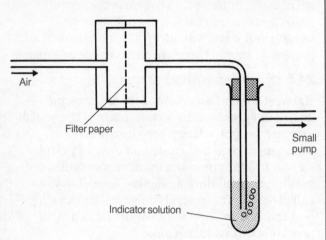

Fig. 24.4 An air pollution investigation

1 The apparatus in Fig. 24.4 could be used to compare the smoke and sulphur dioxide in the air in two different places.

A small pump sucks air through the apparatus. The air passes through a filter paper which traps smoke particles. Then the air passes through a dilute indicator solution. The time is measured until the indicator changes colour.

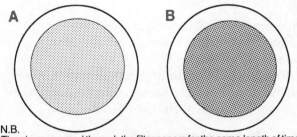

N.B.
The air was passed through the filter papers for the same length of time.

Fig. 24.5 The filter paper after testing in two places

Fig. 24.5 shows the filter papers after testing in two places. Table 24.1 shows the times necessary for the indicator to change colour in the same two places.

Air sample	Time taken for indicator to change colour
	(seconds)
A	95
B	465

Table 24.1 The time necessary for an indicator to change colour in two separate places

(a) Why is it essential to use the same pump in the two experiments?

(b) What must also be the same in each experiment?

THE GROWING PROBLEM OF ACID RAIN

THE ACIDITY of rain falling on Great Britain is increasing and a Government report published yesterday suggested the setting up of a system of monitoring throughout the country.

The problem is most severe in the West Central Highlands of Scotland and in Cumbria. The levels in these places are as high as in Scandinavia, North America or Germany where concern has already been expressed following reductions in fish stocks and damage to trees.

The Government report was compiled by the United Kingdom Review Group on Acid Rain.

Acid rain is produced when fossil fuels such as coal and oil are burnt. Sulphur dioxide and nitrogen dioxide are released into the air and mix with the moisture in the atmosphere. The rain, therefore, contains sulphuric and nitric acids.

Most of the fossil fuels used in the United Kingdom are used by power stations, heavy industry and motor vehicles. The report stated that about 70% of the pollution is caused by sulphur dioxide and the rest by nitrogen dioxide. Not all of the pollution, however, comes from fuels burnt in this country.

The Institute of Terrestrial Ecology, which contributed to the report, has established that increased acidity levels in the East of Scotland can be attributed to winds blowing from the industrial belts of Northern Germany.

It is known that acidity levels are generally higher in the East of the country than in the West. Scientists are, however, unable to explain some freak results. In the South-east readings taken at Tillingbourne and at Bracknell are amongst the highest in the country.

The report calls for the setting up of a co-ordinated national monitoring scheme, especially in remote areas most at risk. Data on acidity levels in urban areas should also be obtained. The Government must commit itself to long-term funding if these recommendations are to be implemented, concludes the report.

It has been calculated that acid rain is costing British farmers at least 25 million pounds per annum. Part of this cost comes from the reduced yields of arable crops. Forestry, in particular, is badly hit. Symptoms of the damage caused by acid rain include death of new shoots, loss of pine needles, browning of foliage and slowing down of the rate of tree growth. There is also incalculable damage to buildings and machinery from acid rain.

Friends of the Earth yesterday condemned as 'utterly inadequate' the Department of the Environment's failure to take action on evidence released in its own official study of acid rain. 'Britain is already the worst acid rain polluter in Western Europe', the organization said in a statement.

The report shows that Britain's rain is up to 150 times more acid than natural rain and becoming increasingly acidic. Also, Britain exports 76% of all sulphur emitted here and this contributes to acid rain pollution in Europe.

10th Jan 1984

(c) What can be concluded from the two experiments?

2 Read the article on the opposite page and answer the questions which follow.

(a) The article mentions three organizations which are concerned with acid rain. Name these three organizations.

(b) Which Government department is responsible for monitoring air pollution?

(c) What are the major users of fossil fuels?

(d) Why is a national policy on acid rain not sufficient to overcome the problem?

(e) Why are acidity levels higher in the East than in the West?

3 Fig. 24.6 shows the levels of ozone in the air in Los Angeles during a day in August 1984.

(a) At what time of day is the ozone level at a maximum?

(b) Why are ozone levels lower at night than during the day?

(c) Explain why the ozone levels change during the day.

4 Read the following newspaper article (below) and answer the questions which follow.

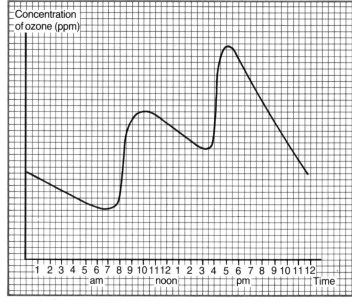

Fig. 24.6 Levels of ozone measured at Los Angeles

(a) Which gas mentioned in the article pollutes the air?

(b) Which substance present in granite produces this radioactive gas?

(c) What building methods are suggested to prevent high levels of the gas in houses?

'CANCER GAS' Build-up in homes

SCIENTISTS and Government building experts are investigating methods of reducing levels of an invisible radioactive gas called radon which builds up naturally in some British homes and can cause lung cancer.

Launching its report on natural radiation and waste disposal yesterday, the National Radiological Protection Board stressed that, although radon is present in every home, it is not a problem in the majority of cases. It would have to be inhaled 'over a very long period' to cause lung cancer.

Methods of reducing radon levels are being investigated. They include a plastic or polythene barrier in the foundations of buildings and sophisticated ventilation systems.

The gas, a product of the natural decay of radium, is most common in granite areas because of the presence of uranium in the stone. High levels of radon have been detected in some parts of Devon and Cornwall, but the number of homes thought to be affected is small.

In its report, the board says that radon 'gently drifting out of the ground everywhere' seeps into houses from underneath or from building materials. 'Natural radiation doses are not always at levels of no concern. Some indoor exposures are high enough to suggest the implementation of control measures.'

When the gas is inhaled, radioactive material is deposited in the respiratory tract. In cases of prolonged exposure this can lead to lung cancer. An earlier estimate suggested that the danger from radon in some parts of South-West England was equivalent to smoking 10 cigarettes a day.

27 January 1984

Activities continued

(d) Why do high levels build up in houses when the amounts in ordinary air are so minute?

6 Read the following article and answer the questions which follow:

(a) Why might alternatives to petrol and diesel oil have to be found?

(b) List the advantages and disadvantages of using hydrogen in an ordinary car engine.

(c) At present some vehicles are electrically powered, e.g. milk floats. Explain briefly how they differ from electric vehicles powered by fuel cells. What drawbacks do present electric vehicles have?

(d) Trolleybuses are to be reintroduced into Bradford. Trolleybuses get their electricity supply from overhead wires. What are the advantages and disadvantages of trolleybuses?

HYDROGEN – A MOTOR FUEL OF THE FUTURE?

A CAR engine uses either petrol or diesel oil and both come from crude oil. There is only a limited amount of the fossil fuel crude oil in the earth and eventually alternative fuels may have to be found.

Hydrogen seems a possible alternative to petrol or diesel oil. It could be obtained from water but at present this is an expensive process.

A given mass of hydrogen could produce three times as much energy as petrol but storage in the vehicle could cause problems.

It would have to be stored either as a gas under pressure or as a liquid under refrigeration.

Hydrogen burns in pure oxygen to form only one product – water. It could therefore be pollution-free.

A normal car engine could be adapted to burn hydrogen. It burns much faster than petrol and so a special carburettor would have to be developed. Also in this engine, because air is used and not oxygen, some oxides of nitrogen would be produced.

Modern technology is developing 'fuel cells' which would directly turn hydrogen and oxygen into water and produce electrical energy very efficiently. This electricity could be used to power electric motors to drive the car 'pollution-free'. The car would be silent and almost maintenance-free. At present, however, the fuel cells cannot produce enough electrical power to drive a car.

Fig. 24.7 A trolleybus

Summary

Sulphur dioxide is regarded as the major polluting gas in the air. Oxides of nitrogen may be as dangerous. Much of the atmospheric pollution is due to combustion of fossil fuels in factories or in motor vehicles.

Answers

Unit 1 Laboratory safety

1 Likely causes of an accident.

(a) Fire exit doors obstructed by a box.
(b) Concentrated acid stored on a narrow, high shelf.
(c) Cupboard door left open.
(d) Bottle of 'pop' in the laboratory.
(e) Water tap left on.
(f) Tripod very near the edge of the bench.
(g) Person on the left picking up a bottle by its neck.
(h) Broken apparatus on the bench.
(i) Wet patch on the floor.
(j) Fire extinguisher is missing.
(k) Poison cupboard left open.
(l) A thermometer is near the edge of the bench.
(m) Curtains hanging near the Bunsen burner.
(n) A stool is left blocking a gangway.

2 Possible dangers.

(a) Bottle of chemical left without a lid.
(b) The observers are not wearing goggles.
(c) Paula has long hair which is not tied back. It could catch alight.
(d) Paula is pointing the test tube at the observers. The chemicals could spit out of the test tube.

3 Perspex is a lot lighter than glass and it does not break easily. The disadvantages of Perspex are that it can get scratched which makes it difficult to see through and if it gets hot it can melt or burn.

4 Protective clothing.
Butcher – apron and cap.
Building worker – safety helmet and shoes with steel toecaps.
Fireman – helmet and oil skins.
Motor cycle rider – crash helmet, leather suit and boots.
Racing car driver – crash helmet, special fireproof suit and overalls.

Unit 2 The Bunsen burner

1 (a) 88 years (1899–1811)
(b) 41 years (1852–1811)
(c) France (Paris), Germany (Berlin) and Austria (Vienna).
(d) Torch and similar dry batteries are carbon zinc batteries.
(e) An antidote is a substance taken to overcome the effects of a poison. If a person has accidentally swallowed arsenic, iron oxide could be swallowed to stop the poison acting.
(f) Bunsen lost an eye in a laboratory accident. You should always wear goggles when doing experiments in the laboratory.

2 (a) base; (b) collar; (c) jet; (d) chimney

3 Your table should look like this:

	Observations	Conclusions
A.	Colourless liquid	Melted or molten wax
B.	Blue flame	Complete burning of wax as there is plenty of air
C.	Yellow luminous flame	Incomplete burning of wax
D.	Blue flame	Again there is plenty of air and the wax burns completely

Table A1

The fuel for a candle is candle wax. The heat from the flame melts the wax and it is the candle wax vapour which burns.

4 The test tube containing petrol can be heated by standing it in a beaker of hot water. No flames are about and so there is no risk of the petrol burning.

5 Fig. A1 shows the piece of Kaowool paper which was held straight up in the Bunsen burner flame. The white portion in the middle is not blackened because this part of the flame is cool. Fig. A2 shows the piece of paper that was held across the flame. Again the middle part is not blackened as this is the cool part of the flame.

6 There are various possibilities. These include coal or coke fires or furnaces or large magnifying glasses which focus the sun's rays (see Fig. 23.5, p. 79).

7 See Fig. A3. The match head must be in the inner blue cone. If it is lifted into the outer cone it would burn immediately. If the end of a glass tube is held in the inner blue cone a small flame will burn at the other end of the tube (Fig. A4).

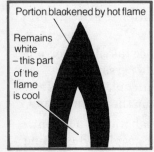

Fig. A1

Fig. A2

Fig. A3

Fig. A4

Unit 3 Chemical apparatus

1   **(i)** Funnel.
    (ii) Mortar and pestle.
    (iii) Teat pipette.
    (iv) Test tube or crucible.
    (v) Small test tube.

2 Conical flask – A general purpose flask which stands on a bench without support.
Flat bottom flask – Again stands on a bench without support. Used when no heat is required.
Side-arm flask – Used for gas preparations and distillations.

Volumetric flask (not used in *Foundation Skills* Volume 1) – A flask used for making up an accurate volume of solution at room temperature.

3 Plastic beakers are cheap to make as they can be easily moulded. They are light and do not break when dropped. Plastic does not react with chemicals.

They are not as easy to see through as glass and they must **not** be heated or they will melt.

4 The markings on the beaker in Fig. 3.1 show the approximate volume when the beaker is filled up to that level. The units are cm^3 or ml (millilitres). These markings are a useful indication of the volume of liquid in the beaker where accurate volumes are not necessary.

5 **(a)** The comparison is fair because the test tubes are all the same size.

  (b) type 1 – £3.75 ÷ 100 approx. 4p
     type 2 – £6.30 ÷ 100 approx. 6p
     type 3 – £19.77 ÷ 100 approx. 20p

  (c) As long as the test tubes themselves do not melt too easily when heated, the teacher should use the cheapest tubes (i.e. type 1).

  (d) 'Pyrex' test tubes can withstand strong heating without melting. They also do not break as easily but, as you have already seen, they are a lot more expensive than the cheap soda glass test tubes. They are made of a special glass.

    'Pyrex' glass is used at home to make glasses, plates, casserole dishes and even saucepans. A hot 'Pyrex' glass dish will not break if it is cooled quickly with cold water.

6 **(a)** A flask could be blown as shown in the photograph 'by hand' or, more likely today, by machine. The flask could be blown to take up the shape of a special 'former' or mould.

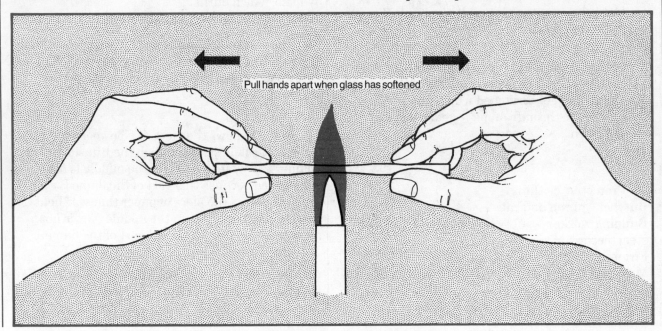

Fig. A5

(b) A teat pipette could be made by heating a piece of glass tubing until the glass softens. The tube is then drawn out so that it becomes narrower by moving the hands apart (see Fig. A5). The tube is taken out of the flame and held until it has cooled. It could then be cut in the middle to produce two teat pipettes.

7 (a) Plastic would not be very suitable for a retort stand because it is not heavy enough and would easily topple over. Also it could melt if accidentally heated.

(b) Plastic is not hard enough to use for making a mortar and pestle.

(c) Plastic is not used for apparatus that needs to be heated and so would be of no use for an evaporating basin.

(d) A spatula could be made of plastic. It is suitable because it is easy to clean and plastic does not react with chemicals.

(e) A trough could be made of plastic although it would need to be fairly strong if it is to hold a lot of water. A plastic trough would be lighter and, therefore, easier to carry.

There are now many different types of plastic. Some can be heated to temperatures of 400°C without melting. These types of plastic are, however, very expensive.

8

Containers	Supporters
CRUCIBLE	STAND
BEAKER	TRIPOD
FLASK	
RETORT	

9 Spatula, stand, crucible, boss, pestle, retort, test tube, gauze, tripod.

10 Some more apparatus mentioned in this book:

Unit 4 Apparatus for measuring

1 An example.

If your room was 400 cm long, 300 cm wide and 250 cm high, its volume would be
$$40 \times 30 \times 25 = 30\,000 \text{ dm}^3$$

2 (a) burette
(b) pipette
(c) measuring cylinder

3 Reasons why you might not get exactly 1000 cm^3 include:

(a) The container might not be completely full.
(b) The container might not be exactly regular in shape.
(c) You might have made an error in measurement or calculation.

Sample results:
A fruit juice container measured 16 cm × 9.5 cm × 6 cm. The volume obtained by multiplying these three together is 988 cm^3. This is a good result.

You can try a similar exercise with a wine box.

4 The pebble would have an irregular shape so that you could not work out its volume by simple measurements. If you partly fill the measuring cylinder with water and note the reading, then drop in the pebble, the water level will rise. Note the new liquid level. The difference between the two readings on the measuring cylinder is the same as the volume of the pebble (see Fig. A6).

You could not use this method to find the volume of a salt crystal because the salt crystal would dissolve in water and disappear. The liquid level would show little or no change.

Apparatus	Made of	Use
Bunsen burner	Metal	Heating
Thermometer	Glass and mercury	Measuring temperature
Gas syringe	Glass (or plastic)	Measuring gas volumes
Burette	Glass	Measuring liquid volumes
Measuring cylinder	Glass or plastic	Measuring liquid volumes
Flasks	Glass	Containers
Goggles	Plastic	Protection of eyes
pH meter	Metal and glass	Measuring pH
Balance	Largely metal	Weighing
Gas jar	Glass	Collecting gases
Beehive shelf	Pottery	Supporting gas jars
Tap funnel	Glass	Separating immiscible liquids
Condenser	Glass	Condensing during distillation
Fractional distillation column	Glass	Aid to separation during distillation
U-tube	Glass	Drying gases
Bell jar	Glass	Holding a large volume of air

Table A2

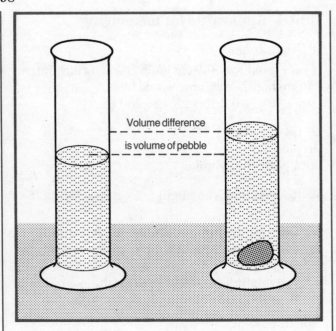

Fig. A6

The same method could be used to find the volume of the salt crystal if another liquid was chosen, e.g. methylated spirit, which did not dissolve the salt crystal.

5 The volumes are only accurate at room temperature because the apparatus itself will change its volume with temperature. It will contract if it is cooled and expand if it is heated. The apparatus is calibrated at room temperature.

6 Measuring cylinder volume $= 54 \text{ cm}^3$
Burette reading $= 3.2 \text{ cm}^3$

7 Burettes are expensive because they are individually made and individually calibrated.

8 It is dangerous to fill a pipette by sucking with your mouth because if you are not very careful you might get some of the chemical into your mouth. Pipettes are often used to measure out volumes of acids and alkalis. Special 'pipette fillers' should be used instead.

9 You could add 2 cm^3 of water from a burette to your test tube and then put one of the rubber bands round the tube where the water level is. Add a further 1 cm^3 of water from the burette and put another rubber band round the test tube at this level. Repeat this again and you will have a test tube which can be used to measure 2, 3 and 4 cm^3 of liquid. You can make the test tube stand up by sticking it into plasticine.

10 Measuring cylinders sometimes have a foam rubber ring around the top so that if they are knocked over, the foam stops the top of the measuring cylinder hitting the bench and breaking.

11 A. 33°C **B.** 94°C
The bath water will be **A**. If you answered **B** you are probably confused about Centigrade and Fahrenheit temperature scales.

12 Thermometers could be designed so that they will not roll off the bench, e.g. they could have a triangular section (see Fig. A7). This might make them more difficult to read.

Fig. A7

The thermometer could be made with reinforced glass for the bulb. It would possibly take longer to give the correct temperature.

During practical work thermometers should be kept in a case if they are not being used.

13 (a) The Bunsen burner flame is far too hot for an ordinary thermometer which only measures up to about 110°C. The mercury will keep expanding and the force of expansion will break the thermometer.

(b) The teacher will want to clear up the remains very quickly because mercury turns to a poisonous vapour in the air. If he or she sprinkles powdered sulphur onto the mercury it removes the mercury.

Unit 5 Weighing

1 Approximate masses:

1p	1.8 g
2p	3.6 g
5p	5.6 g
10p	11.2 g
50p	13.3 g
£1 coin	9.6 g

The bank cashier can tell by weighing a bag of coins how much is in the bag, provided that the coins are not mixed.

2 Errors in weighing.

(a) Balance is not level.
(b) His hands are on the bench.
(c) He has forgotten the lid for the second weighing.

3 Second reading 43.34 g
Third reading 52.75 g

4 If the ether was in an open beaker it would be evaporating quite quickly so that the reading would be going down all the time. In order to obtain an accurate value, the ether would have to be weighed in a closed container, i.e. with a tight fitting lid on.

5 Empty measuring cylinder 110.53 g
   Measuring cylinder + water 150.47 g
   Measuring cylinder + oil 139.75 g
(Oil has a lower density than water)

6 Jane could weigh 100 filter papers and, assuming they all weighed the same, she could divide her answer by 100 to give the mass of 1 filter paper.

Unit 6 Ice, water and steam

1 (a) (i) 20°C
       (ii) 65°C
(b) 3½ minutes
(c) See Fig. A8.
(d) 100°C. The temperature would stay at 100°C after the water had started to boil until the kettle was switched off.

2 (a) In order to make a good cup of tea, the water has to be as hot as possible, preferably boiling, when it is poured onto the tea.
(b) If the pot has been warmed first, the water will stay hotter.
(c) This is also why the teapot should be taken to the kettle. The water will not have time to cool down.
(d) Tea made with water that is not hot enough does not taste very nice.
(e) 7000 metres up Mount Everest water will boil at a lower temperature because of reduced air pressure. This means you cannot make a decent cup of tea there.
(f) The stimulant in tea and coffee is caffeine.

3 (a) If the earth became warmer some of the ice at both poles would melt. This could happen if the earth moved closer to the sun or if more of the sun's rays penetrated the atmosphere.
(b) The amount of water on the earth would increase on the surface of the earth. The level of the oceans would rise and many towns and cities would be submerged.

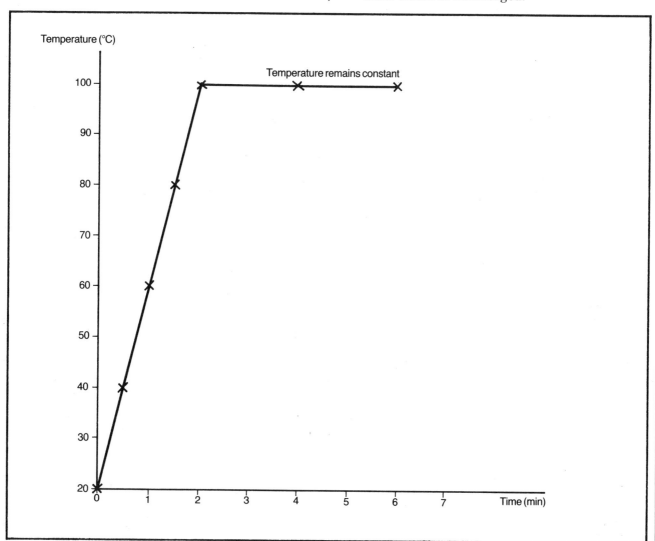

Fig. A8

(c) This in turn would lead to greater evaporation and so more rain.

4 **C** would boil first. Pure water will boil below 100°C if the pressure is reduced. **B** would boil next. Pure water at normal air pressure will boil at 100°C.

A would boil last. Water that contains dissolved substances will boil above 100°C.

5 (a) When the person wearing spectacles enters a hot, steamy kitchen, water vapour from the air will condense on the colder glass lenses of the spectacles and cause them to become misty or 'steamed up'. Plastic lenses are not as cold and the 'steaming up' is much less.

(b) Inside a freezer, water vapour from the air turns to ice on the coldest parts of the freezer. This ice, if melted, would be a sample of pretty pure water.

(c) On a cold morning the window in the bedroom will be cold and water vapour from the warmer air in the bedroom condenses on the cold surface. Warm air can 'hold' more water vapour than cold air.

(d) Puddles dry up because the water evaporates into the air. The evaporation takes place faster on a warmer day because the warm air can 'hold' more water vapour and warm water evaporates quicker than cold water.

(e) On a very cold day the windscreen wash might freeze on the cold windscreen. If it is not quite so cold, spraying the water on the windscreen might cause condensation (misting up) inside the car because of the sudden cooling of the glass.

(f) Water vapour is one of the products of petrol burning. When the engine and car exhaust system is cold this water condenses and turns back to water. This is why in winter, when a car has just been started up, drops of water are seen coming out of the exhaust. Once the engine and exhaust are hot the water comes out of the exhaust as invisible water vapour.

Unit 7 Chemical diagrams

1 See Fig. A9.

2 See Fig. A10.

3 (a) The solid should be in the flask.
(b) The acid should be added carefully, a small amount at a time, through the thistle funnel.
(c) The gas would bubble through the water and collect in the gas jar.
(d) The labels are: Thistle funnel, Flask, Gauze, Tripod, Trough.
(e) Six mistakes are:
   (i) No cork or bung in the flask.
   (ii) Thistle funnel is not long enough. It should dip into the acid in the flask.
   (iii) The liquid in the flask should be level.
   (iv) There should be water in the beehive shelf.
   (v) Unequal levels in the trough.
   (vi) No Bunsen burner as source of heat.

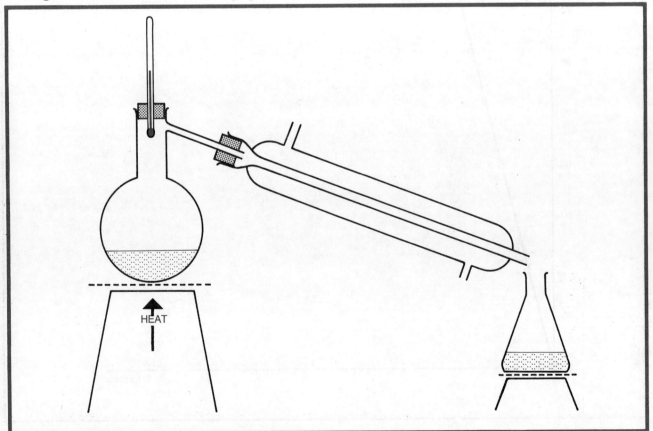

Fig. A10

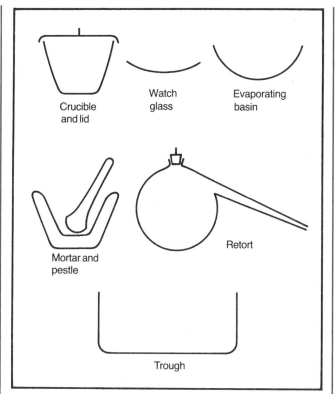

Fig. A9

The correct version of the diagram is shown in Fig. A11.

(f) This method would not be suitable for collecting a dry gas.

Unit 8 Mixing

2 The water does not overflow when the salt dissolves. This suggests that the salt fills spaces between the water particles.

4 A. All the others would make the crystals dissolve quicker.

5 C. The mass of the solution is the sum of the masses of water and salt.

6 (a) Pestle and mortar.

(b) When the mixture of sand and salt is put into the water and the water stirred, the salt will dissolve but the sand will not dissolve and sinks to the bottom of the beaker.

7 The main problem when using a stain-removing liquid to remove a stain is that the solvent might dissolve the material. It is always a good idea to test the solvent on an inside hem to check that it does not affect the material.

9 An emulsion is formed when two immiscible liquids are 'mixed' together so that tiny droplets of one liquid are spread throughout the other liquid.

In milk a small amount of fat is dispersed as tiny droplets throughout the water. This is called an 'oil-in-water' emulsion.

In butter there is a relatively small amount of water dispersed throughout the fat. This is a 'water-in-oil' emulsion.

Unit 9 Filtration and evaporation

1 A sample of rock salt is first crushed and then added to water. The water is stirred to dissolve the salt. Sand and other insoluble impurities sink to the bottom. These impurities can be removed by careful filtering of the mixture.

To obtain the salt from the salt solution some of the water has to be removed. This is done by heating the solution so that the water evaporates. If all the water is evaporated a fine white powder of tiny salt crystals is left. If about half of the water is evaporated away, and the solution left to cool, larger salt crystals will form. These can be separated from the remaining solution by filtering.

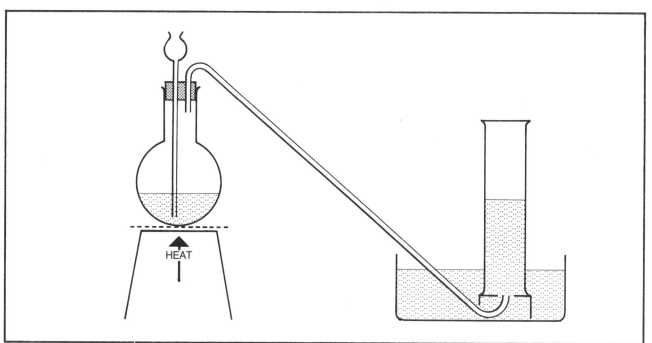

Fig. A11

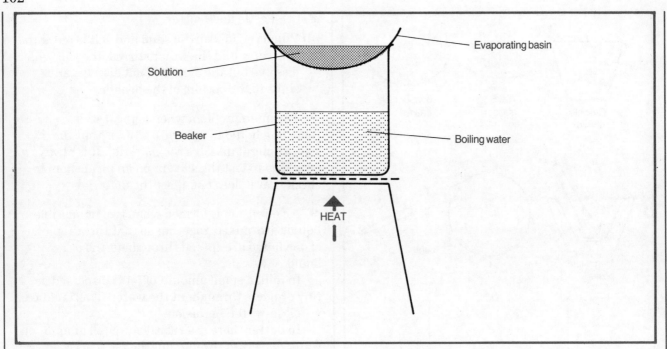

Fig. A12

2 See Fig. A12.

Sometimes evaporating a solution directly over a Bunsen burner causes the solution to evaporate too quickly, resulting in the substance 'spitting' over the bench. Also some chemicals are changed if they get too hot. In both these cases it is often a good idea to evaporate the solution over a 'water bath'. Here the steam heats the evaporating basin and the solution's temperature will not get above 100°C, and the evaporation will be slower.

It is also possible to evaporate a solution slowly by putting it under an infra-red lamp.

3 By stirring the mixture being filtered, Peter might have made a hole in the filter paper and so let some of the solid through. Alternatively he might have stirred the solution so that it came over the top of the filter paper. This would allow some of the mixture to run down between the filter paper and the funnel and thus get into the collecting vessel without passing through the filter paper.

4 An evaporating basin is a fairly shallow dish and so there is always a large surface area of solution in contact with the air. This makes the evaporation faster. The liquid evaporates into a large volume of air.

In a round-bottom flask, although there might be an equally large surface area of solution, the air above the solution cannot move about. It quickly becomes 'saturated' with water vapour. Some of this might condense on the cooler parts of the flask and run back into the solution.

6 (a) The process depends upon the sun evaporating the water from the large shallow beds. In this country there is not enough hot sunshine to satisfactorily evaporate sea water to get salt.

(b) The beds are much better if they are larger and shallow because the larger the surface area of the solution the faster the evaporation will take place.

7 **C**. Dissolving – filtering – evaporating.

8 (a) **C** could be salt because it dissolves in water.

(b) If the mixture is first added to water and stirred, **C** will dissolve. **A** and **B** can be recovered together by filtering. **C** can be obtained from the solution by evaporating.

A and **B** should now be added to petrol and stirred. **A** will dissolve, so **B** can be obtained by filtering.

A can be recovered by careful evaporation of the petrol. A naked flame must not be used.

10

		⁷I		²M		³S	
⁴C	E	N	T	R	I	F	U	G	⁵E
R		S		S		N		V
Y		O		C				A
⁶S	O	L	U	T	I	O	N		P
T		U		B				O
A		B		⁷L	O	⁸W	E	R
L		⁹L	U	T	E		E		A
¹⁰S	¹¹E	E				L		T
	G		¹²R	E	S	I	D	U	E

Fig. A13

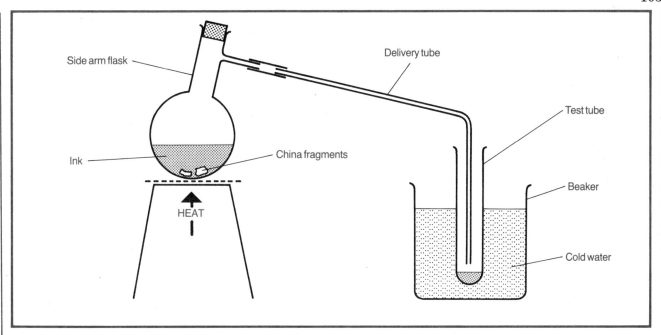

Fig. A14

Unit 10 Distillation

1 (a) See Fig. A14.

(b) You could make more steam condense by putting pieces of ice into the beaker of water. Alternatively, wet filter paper could be wrapped around the delivery tube.

(c) Debra might have let her ink 'boil over' or even have got a drop of the original ink into the side-arm when putting the ink into the flask.

2 The air, even in a desert, contains some water vapour. The air you breathe out contains a lot of water vapour. One suggestion might be to dig a large hole and arrange the plastic sheet so that it covers most of the hole. Weight the centre of the sheet with a stone and put the container underneath the lowest part of the sheet. If you spend the night in the hole water from your breath should condense on the cold plastic sheet and run down into the container. (See Fig. A15.)

4 (a) 23 years old.

(b) Trichloromethane and ethanal.

(c) Obtained on their own in a fairly pure form.

(d) Minerals from the soil. These are taken in solution through the roots of the plant. If these minerals are not replaced in the soil, the soil becomes barren.

(e) Many chemists training in Great Britain learn German because a lot of important research is done in Germany and the results are published in German chemical journals.

5 See Fig. 10.2 (page 31).

6 A Graham condenser is more efficient than a Liebig condenser because the central tube coils round and so is much longer. This means the vapours are surrounded by cold water for longer and therefore are cooled better.

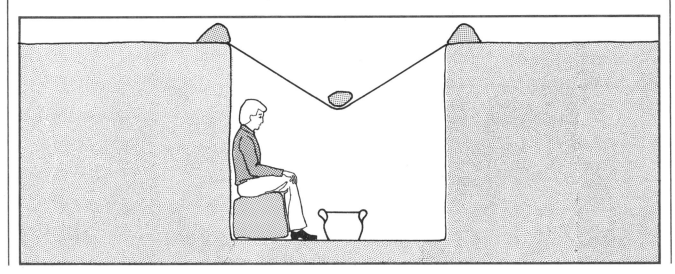

Fig. A15

7

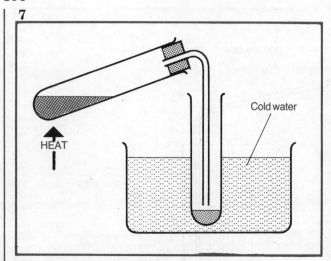

Cold water

HEAT

Fig. A16

8 (a) The energy used to produce the steam is most likely to come from burning oil.

(b) As the pressure goes down, the boiling point of the water also goes down.

(c) The relatively cold sea water is used to cool, and so help to condense, the water vapour in the chambers.

9 A laboratory still is really quite a simple distillation apparatus. Cold water runs up the outer tube to keep the level of water in the boiling compartment unchanged. The water is continuously boiled by electric elements similar to those used in electric kettles.

The steam produced comes down the central tube where it is cooled and condensed by the cold water going up the outer tube. The overflow is necessary to keep the level in the boiling compartment constant.

Distillation in this way is a slow and expensive process.

Unit 11 Fractional distillation

1

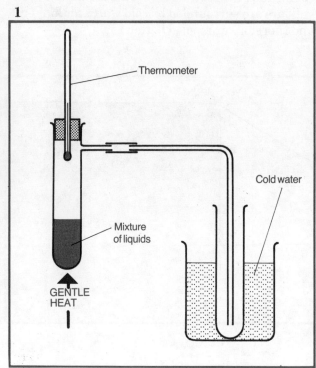

Thermometer

Cold water

Mixture of liquids

GENTLE HEAT

Fig. A17

The apparatus could be set up as shown in Fig. A17. You would have to heat the mixture slowly and carefully. The liquid that boiled at 60°C would boil first. You would have to keep an eye on the thermometer to make sure that the temperature does not go above 60°C. When all the lower boiling point liquid has evaporated, the temperature will rise. Change the receiving test tube so that you can collect a fairly pure sample of the higher boiling point liquid by continuing the heating until the temperature reaches 110°C.

2 (a) 20°C is room temperature.

(b) The first liquid starts to boil after about four minutes. It has a boiling point of 45°C.

(c) The second liquid starts to boil after about seven minutes and has a boiling point of 65°C.

(d) The third liquid starts to boil after about 11 minutes and has a boiling point of 100°C. This liquid could be water.

(e) After seven minutes the thermometer reads 45°C.

(f) The thermometer still shows 20°C after two minutes because, although the mixture has been heated, no vapour has reached the thermometer. The first liquid has a boiling point of 45°C and, until the vapour of this liquid reaches the thermometer bulb, the temperature will not change.

(g) (i) The temperature is greatest at **D** (56°C).
(ii) The temperature is constant at **C** (45°C). This is the boiling point of the first liquid.
(iii) The rate of change of temperature is fastest when the graph is steepest, i.e. at point **B**.

3 The 'proof' system is over 500 years old. It was devised to try and prevent the 'watering down' of alcoholic drinks. A 100° proof solution is a mixture of ethanol and water sufficiently rich in ethanol to set gunpowder alight when a light is applied.

(a) 70° proof is about 40% ethanol (see Fig. A18).

(b) A bottle of wine containing 10% ethanol will be about 18.5° proof (see Fig. A18).

(c) The 'proof strength' of a solution can now be found by measuring the density of the solution.

Unit 12 Chromatography

1 (a) A botanist is a scientist who studies plants.
(b) 31.

(c) This was the time of great unrest in Russia – the Revolution ended in 1917. The First World War was from 1914–1918. Much of the research done at this time did not immediately come to light.

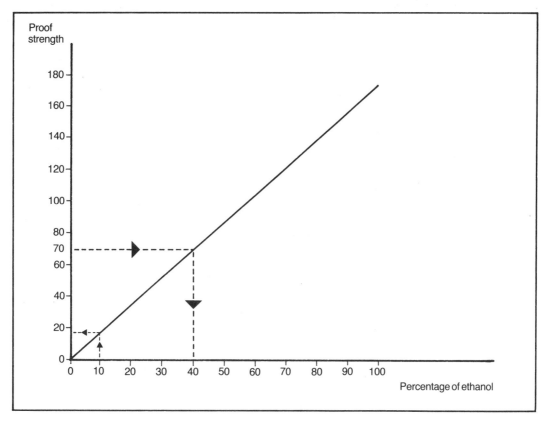

Fig. A18

(**d**) Martin was involved in the development of both paper and gas chromatography.

(**e**) Tswett used petrol as his solvent.

(**f**) Paper chromatography is an easy, quick and reliable method for separating small quantities of material.

2 (**a**) If the blot is below the water level it will 'wash off' into the water and a poor chromatogram will result.

(**b**) Ball point pen inks can be separated in a similar way as long as a suitable solvent is used. Ethanol is a good solvent for ball point inks.

4 By making chromatograms of the two separate felt pens and a chromatogram of the ink used in the letter, the forensic scientist could compare the results and identify the pen used.

5 (**a**) The public analyst could extract the dye from the squash. Then, by simple paper chromatography, he could show that the colour was produced by mixing of certain dyes. By comparison with chromatograms of known dyes he or she could identify the dyes present. Finally a check could be made to see if they were on the 'permitted list'.

6 (**a**) The colours in grass are not soluble in water and so another solvent must be used.

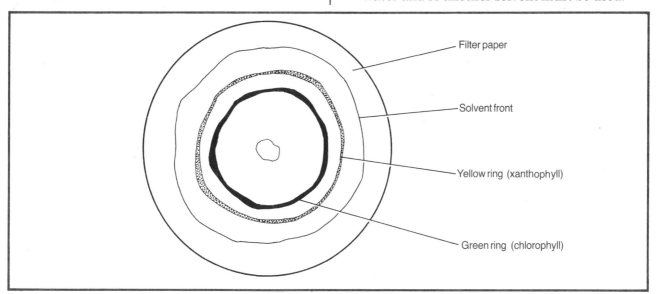

Fig. A19

The dye can be obtained if the grass is cut up and then ground with a small volume of propanone using a mortar and pestle. Finally the coloured solution can be removed by decanting.

(b) (i) Propanone could be used to spread the blot out. Alternatively, ethanol could be used both to extract the dye from the grass and to enlarge the blot.

(ii) (See Fig. A19 on previous page.)

(c)

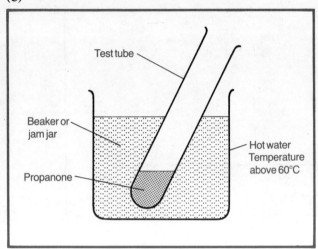

Fig. A20

Unit 13 Sublimation

3 From Table 13.1 we can see that, on heating, ammonium chloride sublimes and the other two chemicals melt. This means that, by using an apparatus similar to the one in Fig. 13.2, the ammonium chloride can be separated from the mixture.

If the chemicals remaining are cooled and then added to water, the potassium chloride will dissolve easily. The urea can be removed by filtering.

Finally, the potassium chloride can be obtained from the solution by evaporation.

Unit 14 Pure substances

1 (a) To assay means to test the purity of a substance. Here the assay is the percentage purity. The results of the test, listing the total impurities present, are also given.

(b) Calcium metal reacts with water and so it must be kept dry. Some metals that react with water are stored in paraffin oil to keep them away from water vapour in the air. This is not normally done with calcium.

(c) It is clearly cheaper to buy calcium in larger quantities but because of its reaction with water and with air it is not easy to store it for long periods. This makes it better to buy small amounts of 'fresh' calcium rather than large amounts.

It is good advice when buying chemicals to buy them in quantities which will not last for longer than one year.

(d) Calcium carbonate occurs naturally in several forms. Two mentioned here are Iceland spar and marble chippings.

(e) (i) Technical grade: calcium oxide

(ii) Laboratory reagent grade:
calcium carbonate powder
calcium hydroxide
calcium chloride

(iii) Analytical reagent grade: calcium carbonate

(f) Calcium chloride hexahydrate is a lot cheaper than calcium, so it is unlikely that it is made from calcium metal.

2 It is never good practice to return unused chemical to a chemical bottle. The unused chemical may have become impure or someone might return it to the wrong bottle. In either case it would spoil the purity of the whole bottle.

Unit 15 Chemicals – where they come from

1 Limestone quarrying can leave huge 'scars' of exposed rock which look ugly and out of place in a beautiful rural landscape. When the quarry has been 'worked out' these cliff faces can be made less severe and covered with top soil so that grass will grow again.

Also quarrying can leave deep holes which fill with water and can be dangerous. These should be filled and again a layer of topsoil added. In some places worked-out quarries have been made into small lakes which can be used for water sports. It is important that the final effect fits in with the surroundings.

The limestone industry can cause other problems in rural areas. Large lorries are needed to transport limestone along what are often fairly narrow roads. Sometimes a railway line has to be laid. Dust and noise can cause problems for local people.

One advantage of the industry is that it provides employment for local people.

2 (a) Re-cycling is the process where used materials are treated so that they can be re-used to make new things. This saves world resources.

(b) Many materials are re-cycled already. These include paper, glass, lead, aluminium ('silver paper' and milk bottle tops) and scrap iron.

(c) The iron and steel can be removed from scrap metal by using a strong magnet. (See Fig. A21.)

Fig. A21

(d) Three non-ferrous metals (i.e. those not containing iron) are copper, brass and aluminium.

(e) Two advantages of this new process are that it is a lot faster and it is more automatic and more efficient at removing metals.

(f) You could show that the hand picking only removes 40% of the non-ferrous metals by putting the rest through the new Warren Spring process to see how much more metal is separated.

3 Composition of rocks from the moon (Fig. A22)

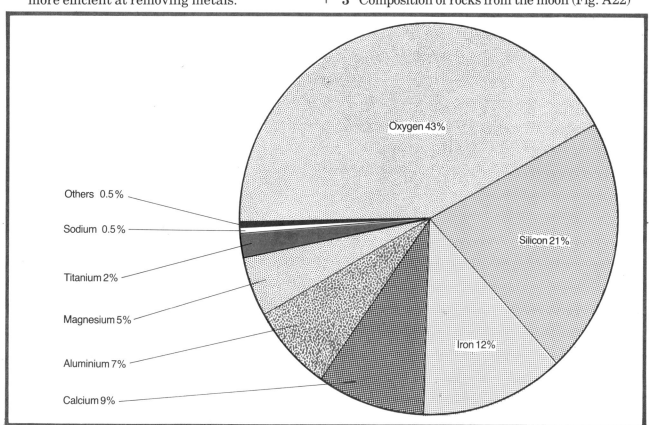

Fig. A22

It is interesting to see that the rock from the moon has a similar composition to rock on earth. Oxygen and silicon make up about two-thirds of the total which is slightly more than in the earth's rocks. Aluminium is the most abundant metal on the earth (8.1%) but iron is the most abundant metal on the moon (12% compared to 5% on earth). Notice that there is five times as much titanium on the moon. Titanium is an increasingly important metal.

4 **(a)** Salt can be obtained from underground deposits as shown in Fig. 15.5 or by dissolving the salt underground. Water is pumped down to where the salt is and, after allowing time for the salt to dissolve, the solution is pumped back to the surface. The solution is then evaporated to produce solid salt. (See Fig. A23.)

This method cannot be used for limestone because limestone does not dissolve in water.

(b) Before the start of salt mining there were no meres. With the removal of salt the ground started to sink or subside. The resulting holes filled with water. Subsidence can also produce other problems (see Fig. A24).

5 All these factors could affect the price of a metal.

(i) The more a metal is in demand by customers the more expensive it is likely to be, especially if the supply cannot easily meet the demand. You will find the current market prices for metals in the financial columns of a daily newspaper.

(ii) If the metal occurs in fairly large quantities in the earth it is likely to be cheaper.

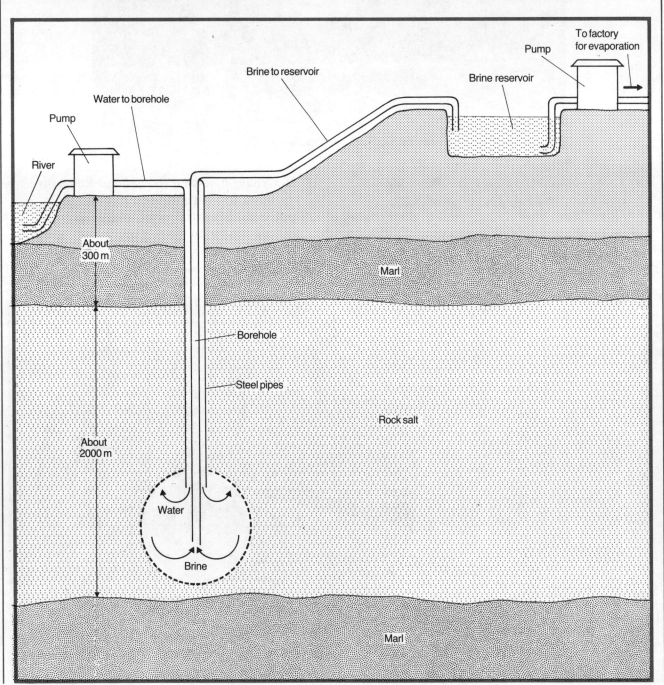

Fig. A23

Fig. A24

(iii) The difficulty of extraction will influence the price. Metals which require a great deal of electricity to extract them are expensive.

The price of a metal is determined by a combination of factors.

6 Tin mines were abandoned in Cornwall because fairly large amounts of a rich, easily extracted ore were found in Malaysia. Tin from here was also cheaper because of lower labour costs.

The tin mines in Cornwall might be re-opened if

 (i) deposits in Malaysia run out;
 (ii) Malaysian tin becomes very expensive;
(iii) political problems affect the supply;
(iv) the demand for tin, and hence the price, increase;
 (v) cheaper methods of mining and extracting the tin in Cornwall can be found.

Unit 16 Acids and alkalis

 3 (a) Blue.
(b) 4–6.
(c) Green (a mixture of blue and yellow).

4 This series of colours is found in the same order as in the rainbow produced when white light is split up by raindrops.

5 (a)

Liquid	Colour with litmus	Colour with universal indicator	pH
A	Red	Red	1
B	Blue	Purple	13
C	Purple	Green	7
D	Red	Orange	5
E	Purple	Green	7

Table A3

(b) **(i)** hydrochloric acid – tube **A** – strong acid.
 (ii) ethanoic acid – tube **D** – weak acid.
 (iii) sodium hydroxide – tube **B** – strong alkali.

(c) Water or salt solution is neutral so could be in tubes **C** and **E**.

(d) You could measure the density of each solution. Salt water will have a density of more than 1 g/cm^3. Water should have a density of 1 g/cm^3 at room temperature.

Another way would be to evaporate a small amount of each solution on a watch glass over a water bath. When all the liquid has evaporated you could easily tell the difference. In the case of pure water no residue would remain. With salt solution a solid residue of salt should remain. It is unwise, of course, to taste either liquid.

6   **(i)** The reading on the pH meter is 5.6.
   (ii) This means the solution is weakly acidic.
   (iii) In order to make a solution of pH 2 by adding another chemical to **X** you would have to add a strong acid, i.e. hydrochloric acid.

Unit 17 Neutralization

2 You will see fizzing when the two chemicals are mixed. A colourless gas is produced. We call this fizzing effervescence.

4 **(a)** To show that a 'stinging nettle' contains an acid you could grind up a few nettle leaves in a pestle and mortar with a small volume of water. The mixture can then be warmed in a boiling tube. The solution is removed by decantation.

    Finally, the solution could be tested with universal indicator paper.

(b) If the 'stinging nettle' contains an acid and relief can be obtained by rubbing on a 'dock leaf' on the sting, it suggests that the 'dock leaf' must contain a chemical which overcomes the acid, i.e. an alkali which neutralizes the acid.

5 Plants suited to acid soils and alkaline soils.

Acid soil	Alkaline soil
Rhododendron	Cherry
Azalea	Juniper
Lavender	Laburnum
Wallflowers	Lilac
Stocks	Birch
Heather	Broom
Hydrangea	Holly

Table A4

6 **(a)** The dye in the stain was acting as an indicator. It was one colour when acid or neutral and a different colour when made alkaline by adding soap.

(b) If vinegar (a weak acid) had been added to the dye after it was treated with soap, it should have changed the dye back to its original colour.

(c) You could try a commercial 'stain remover' or carefully try another solvent other than water, e.g. ethanol.

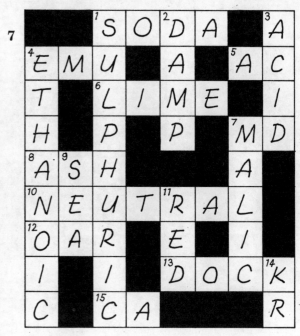

Fig. A5

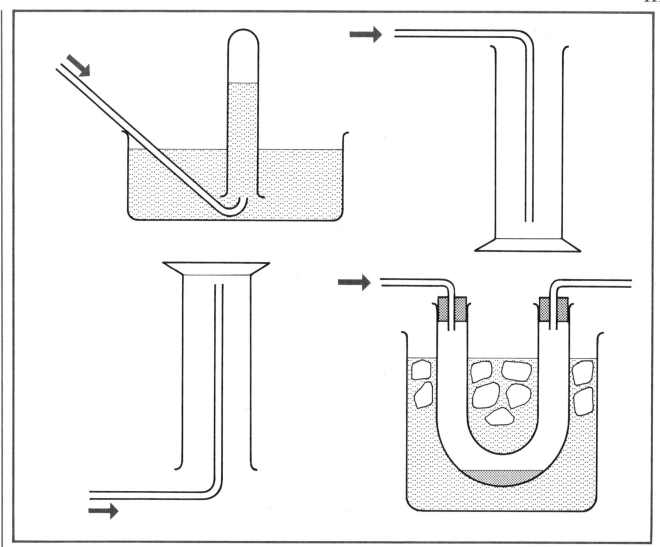

Fig. A26

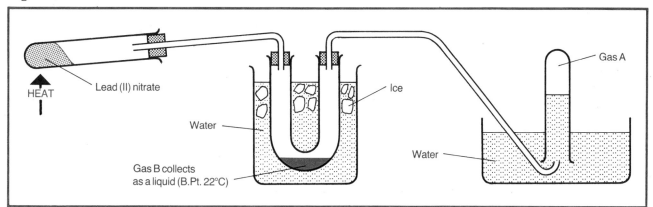

Fig. A27

Unit 18 Collecting gases

1 See Fig. A26.

2 If a piece of moist red litmus paper is held near the bottom of the inverted gas jar, the litmus paper will turn blue when the gas jar is full of ammonia.

3 See Fig. A27.

4 Assuming that a gas was given off when the solid was heated, the gas must have gone somewhere if none was collected. If there were no leaks in the apparatus then the gas must have dissolved in the water.

5 (a) Hydrogen sulphide is quite soluble in cold water, so it cannot be collected in this way. However, from the table you can see that it is almost insoluble in hot water. You can still collect it over water providing it is hot water.

(b) Hydrogen sulphide has a similar density to air so it is difficult to collect by upward or downward delivery. If a dry sample is needed it could be collected in a gas syringe.

Unit 19 Heating Common Substances

1

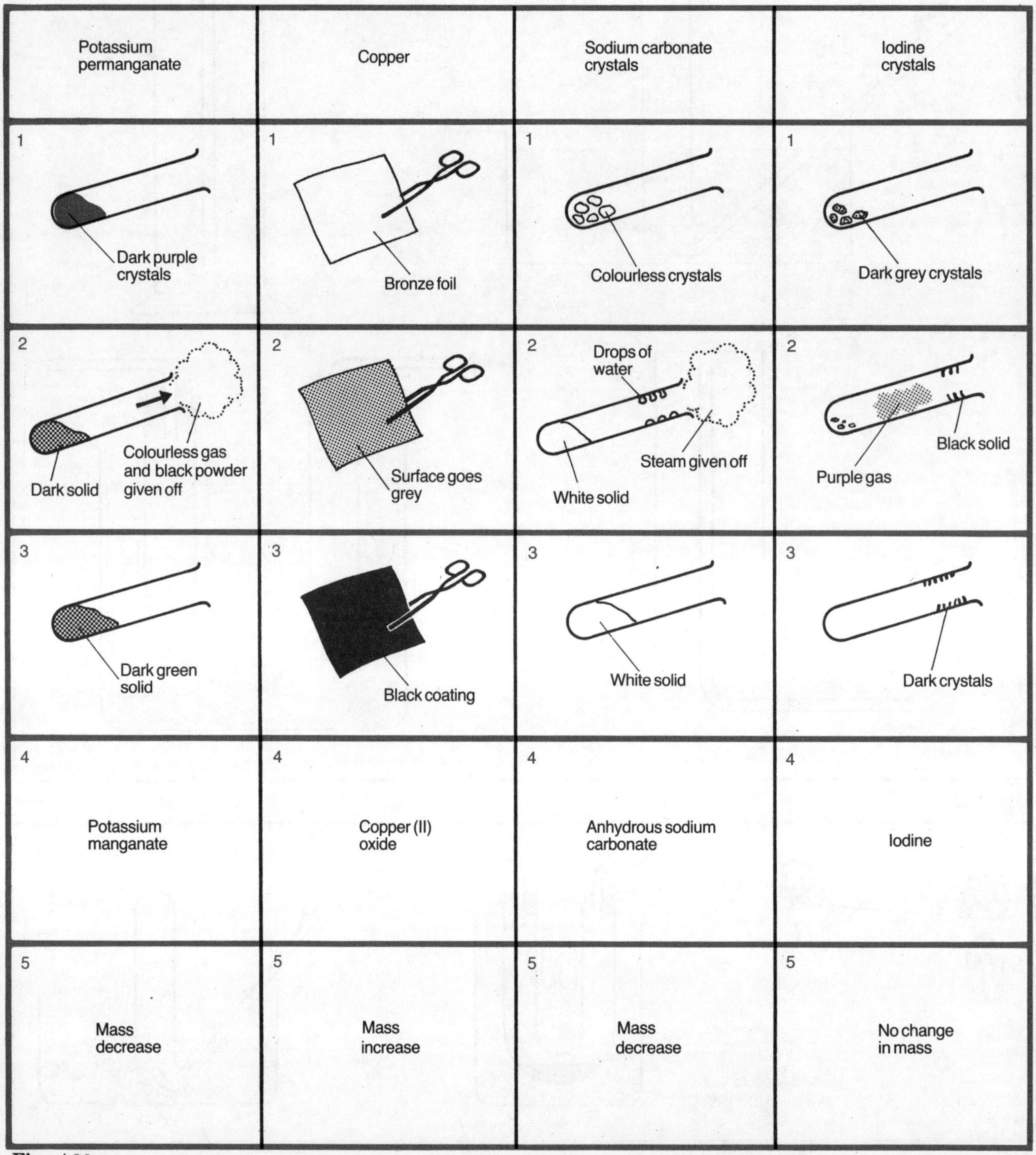

Potassium permanganate	Copper	Sodium carbonate crystals	Iodine crystals
1 Dark purple crystals	1 Bronze foil	1 Colourless crystals	1 Dark grey crystals
2 Dark solid — Colourless gas and black powder given off	2 Surface goes grey	2 Drops of water — Steam given off — White solid	2 Purple gas — Black solid
3 Dark green solid	3 Black coating	3 White solid	3 Dark crystals
4 Potassium manganate	4 Copper (II) oxide	4 Anhydrous sodium carbonate	4 Iodine
5 Mass decrease	5 Mass increase	5 Mass decrease	5 No change in mass

Fig. A28

Substances from Fig. 19.1 or 19.2 which resemble these are:

Potassium permanganate – red lead
Copper – magnesium
Sodium carbonate crystals – copper(II) sulphate crystals
Iodine crystals – ammonium chloride

2 (i) Sand is unchanged.
  (ii) Ammonium chloride sublimes.
  (iii) Magnesium is heated in a crucible.

3 (i) The lid is on the crucible to stop any smoke or ash escaping. This allows any mass change to be measured accurately.

(ii) It is necessary to lift the lid from time to time to let air into the crucible so that the magnesium will burn.

4

Permanent changes on heating	Temporary changes on heating
Red lead	Sulphur
Magnesium	Zinc oxide
	Copper(II) sulphate
	Cobalt(II) chloride
	Ammonium chloride

Table A6

5

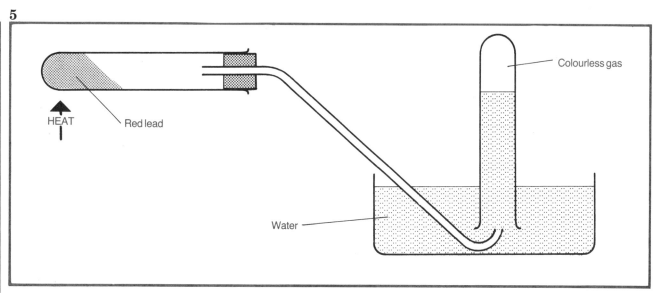

Fig. A29

6 (i) Anhydrous copper(II) sulphate must be kept in a well-stoppered bottle in order to keep the moisture in the air away from it.

(ii) When anhydrous copper(II) sulphate reacts with water it turns to its original blue colour. Water is the only liquid that will turn anhydrous copper(II) sulphate blue. This reaction can be used as a test to see if a liquid contains any water. It is not a test for *pure* water.

7 (i) After dipping the filter paper in cobalt(II) chloride solution it would be pink.

(ii) After drying the paper in an oven it would be royal blue.

(iii) Cobalt(II) chloride paper is used to test for water.

8 Experiment (i) showed that the copper wire turns black when it is heated by electricity. This suggests that the black is not soot from a flame.

Experiment (ii) showed that when a copper wire is heated in the absence of air it does not go black. This suggests that the air has something to do with it going black.

Experiment (iii) showed that when a copper wire is heated in a sealed tube out of contact with air it does not go black.

These results lead us to the conclusion that the black coating is not soot from the flame but is caused by a reaction of the copper with part of the air. This is further supported by the fact that copper gains mass when it turns black. The black coating is copper(II) oxide formed when copper reacts with oxygen from the air.

This oxide can only form on the surface and so there is only a very small change in mass. In the case of magnesium, the magnesium burns and all the magnesium is changed to magnesium oxide, not just a surface coating, and so there is a greater increase in mass.

9 (a) Tungsten is used as a filament in light bulbs because it has a very high melting point.

(b) If air was present inside the light bulb, the oxygen would combine with the tungsten at the very high temperatures reached. The filament would break.

Unit 20 Air and its composition

1 (a) Nitrogen makes up nearly 80% of the air.
(b) Xenon has the highest boiling point (−108°C).
(c) Neon and helium would still be gases at −200°C.
(d) The noble gases make up nearly 1% of the air. Every time you breathe, you take in 5 cm³ of noble gases. Argon itself makes up 0.9% of the air so that it can hardly be considered as a rare gas. The term 'rare gases' is not therefore a good name and 'noble gases' is now widely used.

2 (i) Figs. 20.6(a) and (b) show oxygen in use and Figs. 20.7(a) and (b) show nitrogen in use.
(ii) Fig. 20.6(a) shows oxygen being given to a patient during an operation and Fig. 20.6(b) shows an oxygen lance being used to introduce more oxygen into a furnace. Fig. 20.7(a) shows nitrogen being used to freeze the inside of golf balls so that the elastic layer can be wound on without distortion. Fig. 20.7(b) shows nitrogen being used to freeze meat pasties.

4 (a) 20 cm³ of gas were used up in the experiment.
(b) The gain in mass of the hard glass tube and copper was 0.027 g (59.272 g − 59.245 g).
(c) The gas used must have had a mass of 0.027 g.
  20 cm³ of the gas has a mass of 0.027 g
  1 cm³ of the gas has a mass of 0.00135 g
  1000 cm³ of the gas has a mass of 1.35 g
  From Table 20.2, this suggests that the gas is oxygen.

Unit 21 Processes involving air

1 (a) Magnesium oxide is formed when magnesium burns in air.

(b) The lid must be lifted from time to time to let more air into the crucible so that the magnesium can burn.

(c) and **(d)** See Fig. A30.

(e) Group 5's results do not fit the straight line and so are inaccurate.

  If 0.11 g of magnesium had been burned 0.183 g of residue would have been formed.

2 (a) The candle should go out after 88 seconds.

(b) The results do not fall exactly on the line due to inaccuracies in the investigation. Timing would be difficult and it would be impossible to make sure that the candle was burning as well each time. The graph illustrates one important point about graphs in Science compared with graphs in Mathematics. In Mathematics, the points are exact and the graph should go through every point. In Science, there are errors in the position of the points and the graph should go close to, but not necessarily through, each point.

(c) As the volume of air trapped under the beaker increases the time for the candle flame to go out *increases*.

(d) The larger the volume of trapped air there is the more oxygen there is. This means that it will take longer for the candle to use up the oxygen.

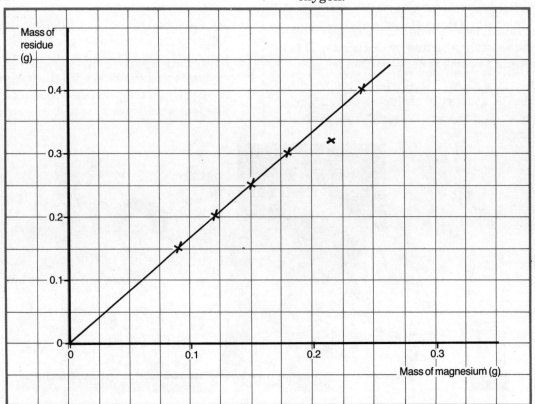

Fig. A30

115

3 (a) The increase in mass was 0.30 g (132.65 g − 132.35 g).
(b) The increase of mass was caused by the soda lime absorbing carbon dioxide or water vapour, or both.
(c) To show that the increase was caused by the candle burning and not just by air, the experiment should be repeated without lighting the candle and then comparing the results. Claire knew that there is some carbon dioxide and water vapour in the air.
(d) When the investigation was done with the candle burning, the increase in mass of the apparatus was a lot quicker than when the experiment was done without lighting the candle.

4 Carbon dioxide reacts with limewater.

5 When iron is in contact with copper the iron 'rots' away faster.

6 The methods of trying to prevent rusting include:
(a) using stainless steel;
(b) painting;
(c) galvanizing (coating with zinc);
(d) special rustproofing, e.g. phosphating.

7 To provide extra oxygen dissolved in the water for fish to breathe.

8 (a) Green plants produce oxygen by photosynthesis.
(b) If all the rain forests were destroyed by fire the amount of oxygen in the air would get less.

The amount of carbon dioxide would increase. Because of the severe reduction in the number of green plants photosynthesis would be greatly reduced. The extra carbon dioxide would produce a heating of the earth by intrapping the heat (this is called the 'greenhouse effect'). The rise in temperature would cause melting of ice caps, etc.

Unit 22 Oxygen

1 (a) See Fig. A31.
(b) The first couple of test tubes of gas collected failed to ignite the glowing splint because they were filled with air displaced from the apparatus.
(c) The manganese(IV) oxide could be recovered from the flask at the end of the experiment by filtering the mixture. It should be washed with distilled water and dried.

2 The hydrogen peroxide bottle probably exploded because of pressure inside the bottle caused by oxygen being produced as the hydrogen peroxide split up.
This splitting up (or decomposition) is speeded up by bright sunlight. It would be best to store hydrogen peroxide in a dark bottle.

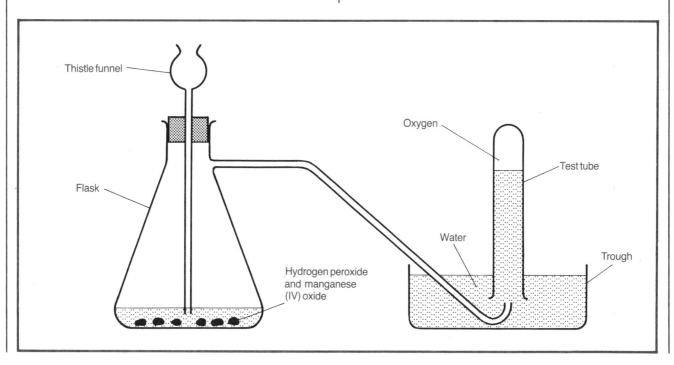

Fig. A31

3

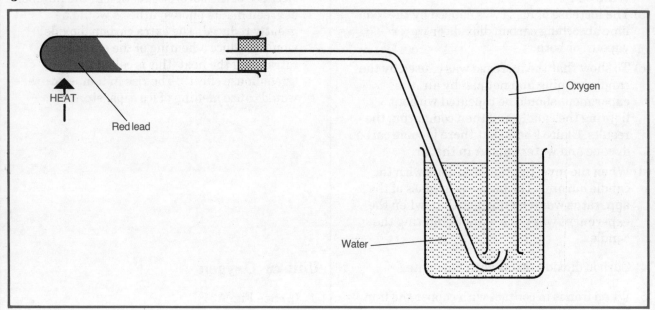

Fig. A32

4 Bubbles of a colourless gas are produced. This gas is oxygen. Liver contains a catalyst which speeds up the decomposition of hydrogen peroxide.

5

Fig. A33

Unit 23 History of the discovery of oxygen

1 (a) (i) 39 **(ii)** 40 **(iii)** 71

(b) Priestley experimented with oxygen, nitrogen and carbon dioxide.

(c) Priestley could see oxygen being important in treating people with breathing problems.

3 (a) (i) 23 **(ii)** 35 **(iii)** 51

(b) The streets were dark and dangerous places at night and Lavoisier considered lighting a large town as a very important project.

(c) You are unlikely to see Lavoisier's experiments repeated in your school laboratory because of the very poisonous properties of mercury vapour and the very large amount of expensive mercury used. Also apparatus and heating methods have changed since 1750. Lavoisier's experiments also take several days.

Unit 24 Air pollution

1 (a) It is essential that the same pump is used in each case to ensure that air is passed through the apparatus at the same rate in both cases.

(b) The volume of indicator should be the same in both cases.

(c) The results of the two experiments show that sample **A** contains much more smoke (more trapped on filter paper – Fig. 24.5) and more polluting gases, e.g. sulphur dioxide, as the indicator changes colour faster (Table 24.1). Sample **B**, which is much less polluted, takes much longer to change the indicator.

This apparatus is similar to the one used for official testing but a more accurate method of measuring the acidity of the solution is used.

2 **(a)** Three groups concerned about 'acid rain' mentioned in the article are:
  (i) The United Kingdom Review Group on Acid Rain;
  (ii) The Institute of Terrestrial Ecology;
  (iii) Friends of the Earth.

(b) The Government department responsible for monitoring air pollution is the Department of the Environment.

(c) The largest users of fossil fuels are power stations, heavy industry and motor vehicles.

(d) A national policy on acid rain is not sufficient to overcome the problem because it is an international problem as well. Polluted air from this country is reputedly causing acid rain in Scandinavia and air pollution from German heavy industry is blown into neighbouring countries.

(e) Acidity levels are higher in the East of England because, with prevailing winds coming from the West, they bring little air pollution from over the sea. Also there is much greater annual rainfall in the West and any air pollution is diluted.

3 **(a)** Ozone levels are highest at about 5.00 p.m.

(b) Ozone levels are lower at night because sunlight is required to produce ozone from the polluting gases.

(c) The ozone levels are at the greatest at or just after the 'rush-hour traffic'. Many of the polluting gases are produced by petrol engines.

4 **(a)** Radon is the polluting gas mentioned in this article.

(b) The substance present in granite rock is uranium. This decays to radium which in turn produces radon. It is a very slow process, taking millions of years, and therefore radon levels are normally low.

(c) In order to prevent the build-up of radon in houses, the article suggests using a plastic or polythene barrier in the foundations and to have sophisticated ventilation systems.

(d) Radon builds up in houses by seeping in from the ground or from out of the building materials. This is not normally a problem in the open air as the gas is readily dispersed.

5 **(a)** Alternatives to petrol and diesel oil will have to be found because these fossil fuels will eventually run out. North Sea oil is only expected to last for about 30 years.

(b) The main advantage of hydrogen as a fuel in a car engine is that for the same mass it produces more energy. If the hydrogen burns only in oxygen it produces only water vapour and therefore no pollution. The main disadvantage is the storage of the hydrogen in the vehicle. It could either be stored under high pressure in gas cylinders or refrigerated as a liquid.

(c) Milk floats run off storage batteries. These need to be 'charged up' overnight by plugging into the electricity supply. These vehicles require a number of batteries which are heavy. Also the vehicles can only travel relatively short distances before they are recharged.

In a fuel cell electricity is not stored but produced as required, efficiently, using a chemical reaction.

(d) The advantages of trolleybuses include:
  (i) they produce no pollution;
  (ii) they do not use expensive fossil fuel;
  (iii) they do not carry any fuel;
  (iv) they are very quiet in operation;
  (v) they require much less maintenance.

The disadvantages include:
  (i) they can only run on scheduled routes and cannot be re-routed to avoid traffic congestion;
  (ii) expensive overhead cables must be erected and maintained. These cables are prone to damage and vandalism in a city;
  (iii) in the event of a breakdown the trolleybus cannot easily be moved.

During the 1950s, in particular, the disadvantages outweighed the advantages. Circumstances have changed and trolleybuses may come back in certain places. There is no intention to bring trolleybuses back to London.

118

Glossary

The following words may be met during your Chemistry lessons.

A

Absolute temperature There is a minimum temperature below which it will never be possible to cool anything. This is called **absolute zero** and is −273°C. This is the starting point for the **Kelvin**, or absolute, temperature scale: e.g. 0°C is the same as 273K which is called the absolute temperature.

Acid A substance that dissolves in water to form a solution with a pH below 7. An acid contains hydrogen which can be replaced by a metal to form a salt. The three common mineral acids are sulphuric acid, hydrochloric acid and nitric acid.

Alkali A base that dissolves in water to form a solution with a pH above 7. Alkalis are neutralized by acids to form salts.

Allotropy When an element can exist in two or more forms in the same physical state it is said to show allotropy. The different forms are called **allotropes**. Diamond and graphite are two solid allotropes of carbon.

Alloy A metal made by mixing two or more metals together, e.g. brass is an alloy of copper and zinc.

Amalgams Many metals form alloys when mixed with mercury. These alloys are called amalgams. The mixture used to fill teeth is an amalgam.

Amorphous Without definite or regular shape.

Anhydride An anhydride (sometimes called an acid anhydride) is an oxide of a non-metal which dissolves in water to form an acid.

Anhydrous A substance without water. Often used to describe salts which have lost water of crystallization.

Aqueous solution A solution made by dissolving a substance in water.

B

Base A substance which reacts with an acid to form a salt and water only. A soluble base forms an alkaline solution.

Battery A battery is a source of electricity. A carbon-zinc battery is the type of battery used in a torch. The battery in a car is a lead-acid battery which stores electricity.

Boiling When a liquid turns rapidly to its vapour at a fixed temperature called the **boiling point**. The boiling point of a liquid varies with pressure. The lower the pressure the lower the boiling point.

C

Calorimeter Apparatus used for measuring heat.

Catalyst A substance which alters the rate of a chemical reaction but is not used up in the reaction.

Chemical change A change which results in the formation of new substances. A chemical change is not easily reversed.

Chromatography A way of separating mixtures, especially of coloured substances, by letting them spread across filter paper or through a powder.

Condensation When a vapour turns to a liquid on cooling. Heat is given out during this change. Condensation is the opposite of evaporation.

Crystal A piece of substance that has a definite, regular shape.

D

Decomposition A chemical reaction that results in the breaking down of substances into simpler ones. This is often brought about by heating.

Density The mass of a particular volume of a substance. It is expressed as kg/m^3 or g/cm^3.

Distillation A way of purifying a liquid or obtaining the solvent from a solution. The liquid is vaporized and the vapour condensed to re-form the liquid. The condensed liquid is called the **distillate**.

Dissolving When a substance is added to water it can disappear from view when stirred. This disappearance is called dissolving. The substance is still there and can be recovered by evaporation.

E

Environment The surroundings in which we, other animals and plants live. A person who studies the environment may be called an **environmentalist**.

Evaporation The process where a liquid changes to its vapour. This happens at a temperature below its boiling point but is at its fastest when the liquid is boiling.

Extraction The removal of one thing from a group of other things.

F

Filtrate The liquid that comes through the filter paper during filtration.

Filtration A method of separating a solid from a liquid. The solid is 'trapped' in the filter paper and the liquid runs through.

Flammable Describing a substance, e.g. petrol, that catches fire easily.

Fractional distillation A method of separating a mixture of different liquids that mix together. The process depends upon the different boiling points. The liquid with the lowest boiling point boils off first and is condensed. As the temperature is raised liquids with higher boiling points distil over.

Freezing When a liquid changes to a solid. It will do this at the freezing point. A pure substance will have a definite freezing point.

Fuel A substance that burns easily to produce heat and light. A **fossil fuel** is present in the earth in only limited amounts and cannot be readily replaced, e.g. coal.

Funnel A piece of glass or plastic apparatus used for filtering. A Buchner funnel is a particular type of funnel usually made of china. It produces quicker filtration because the filtrate is sucked through the filter paper.

H

Hydrated Contains water.

I

Immiscible Two liquids that do not mix are said to be immiscible, e.g. oil and water.

Indicator A chemical that can distinguish between an alkali and an acid by changing colour, e.g. litmus.

Insoluble Describing a substance that will not dissolve in a particular solvent.

M

Melt A solid changes to a liquid at the **melting point**.

Mineral A naturally occurring substance of which rocks are made.

Mixture A substance made by just mixing other substances together. The substances can easily be separated again.

N

Neutralization A reaction where an acid is cancelled out by a base or alkali.

P

pH A measure of the acidity or alkalinity of a solution. The scale is from 0 to 14. Numbers less than 7 represent acids; the smaller the number the stronger the acid. Numbers greater than 7 represent alkalis; the larger the number the stronger the alkali. pH 7 is neutral.

Properties A description of a substance and how it behaves. Physical properties include density and melting point. Chemical properties describe chemical changes.

Pollution The presence in the environment of substances which are harmful to living things.

Precipitate An insoluble substance formed in a chemical reaction. This usually causes a cloudiness to appear in the liquid and eventually the solid sinks to the bottom.

Product A substance formed in a chemical reaction.

Pure substance A single substance that contains nothing apart from the substance itself. Pure substances have definite melting and boiling points.

R

Reactant A chemical substance which takes part in a chemical reaction.

Residue The insoluble substance left on a filter paper during filtration.

S

Salt A substance which is formed as a product of a neutralization reaction.

Saturated solution A solution in which no more of the solute will dissolve providing the temperature remains unchanged.

Solute The substance that dissolves in a solvent to form a solution.

Solvent The liquid in which a solute dissolves.

Sublimation When a solid changes straight from a gas to a solid *or* solid to a gas, missing out the liquid.

Suspension A mixture of a liquid and an insoluble substance where the insoluble substance does not sink to the bottom but stays evenly divided throughout the liquid.

V

Vapour A vapour is a gas that will condense to a liquid on cooling to room temperature.

Viscous A viscous liquid is thick and 'treacle-like'. It is difficult to pour.

Volatile Describes a liquid which is easily turned to a vapour, e.g. petrol.

W

Water of crystallization A definite amount of water bound up in the crystals.

Further reading

1 *Development of the Chemical Balance* by John T. Stock. Published by HMSO.
2 *Scales and Balances* by J.T. Graham. Published by Shire Publications.

These two books give good information about the development of balances.

3 *Discovering Lost Mines* by Peter Taylor. Published by Shire publications.

This book gives information about where you can go to find old mine workings. It can provide some interesting days out.

Organizations supplying interesting information for background reading

The Department of the Environment, Warren Springs Laboratory, Stevenage, Hertfordshire. (Information on air pollution.)

Your local council's Environmental Health Officer. (Information on local air pollution.)

The National Society for Clean Air, 136 North Street, Brighton, BN1 1RG.

Friends of the Earth, 377 City Road, London, EC1V 1NA.

Health and Safety Executive, P.O. Box 109, Maclaren House, 19 Scarbrook Road, Croydon, Surrey, CR9 1QH.

Britoil p.l.c., 150 St Vincent Street, Glasgow, G25 5LJ.

Esso U.K. p.l.c., Victoria Street, London, SE1 5JW.

Cement Makers' Federation, Terminal House, 52 Grosvenor Gardens, London, SW1W 0AH.

Places worth a visit

1 Science Museum, Exhibition Road, London, SW7.
Open 10.00–18.00 Monday–Saturday, 14.30–18.00 Sunday. A wide variety of exhibits including fine galleries devoted to chemical exhibits. Free lectures and films.
2 Geological Museum, Exhibition Road, London, SW7. Open 10.00–18.00 Monday–Saturday, 14.30–18.00 Sunday. The Story of the Earth exhibition, rocks and minerals.
3 Lion Salt Works Ltd., Marston, Northwich, Cheshire, telephone (0606) 2066. Salt is a vital chemical raw material and a working salt works can be seen here.
Open May–September 14.00–17.00 every day.